MANAGING RENTAL PROPERTIES

Beginners Guide to Maximize Profits with Minimal Frustration Utilizing Effective Strategies

Cameron Malone

TABLE OF CONTENTS

Introduction

It doesn't matter whether you own a stand-alone house, duplex apartment, a triplex, or multi-dwelling unit, if you put it up for rent, it means you are a property owner. As a property owner, you need to be well informed. This book starts with the fundamentals and unravels various other steps as you continue to read. It is focused largely on property owners freshly entering the business. It makes managing the returns from your investments easier.

Perhaps you obtained this book with plans to buy your first estate for rent. Or maybe you have unexpectedly purchased an estate that is being leased out presently or will have to be leased out in the future. You may have obtained a rental property as a surprise, through unexpected means. As a matter of fact, the majority of estate owners become property owners the moment they get reassigned to a new location for work.

Whether you accept this as true or not, a lot of individuals who buy and run their own rental properties enjoy it. In the long run, you may perhaps grow your management business and from there start managing other people's estates alongside your own. Deciding to follow that path will more than likely require you to obtain a permit depending on your business location. Since you will be judged based on the high standards of the local, state and federal laws, you must, therefore, have a vast knowledge about the legalities attached to renting out estates. No matter how many estates you oversee, you must constantly maintain them.

Regardless of your situation, you need to have a thorough knowledge of estate management. This book also provides answers to most of your pressing questions. Taking up this book to read, writing down important points, and applying the recommended techniques, will make you more advanced than most property owners.

Chapter 1

Understanding Rental Property Management

One thing is certain, making up one's mind to buy an estate and being able to properly manage that choice is not simple. You must pay equal attention to becoming an estate owner as you would a new business, which you may know nothing about running. When you become an owner of a rental property, there are basic things you must know in order to not get into trouble.

You must show a keen interest in learning some fundamental things from the onset and persist in this vein. Be aware that you will commit a good number of errors. When that happens, pick yourself up, learn from your mistakes, and promise yourself never again to allow such mistakes to replay. At this point, it would be of high recommendation that you join a group with those of the same or similar goals wherein you can receive support as well as learn from other people's experiences.

Understanding the Advantages and Disadvantages

Below is an overview of the pros and cons of buying and overseeing a rental property.

Advantages of Managing a Rental Estate

The advantages of renting out an estate (a lot of which applies whether you employ the services of an estate management company or not) include the following:

- You are the owner of your company.

- You should never become tired of it.

- You don't have to pay for the charges of an expert estate manager.

- Managing your own estate will be easier than what it used to be before current technological advancements.

- It's a public-oriented business.

- It can be both interesting and difficult.

- You may like it enough to make a career out of it and begin managing other people's estates.

- After you have gone past the basic arrangements, there isn't much work from then on.

- Being completely or partially involved is your personal choice.

- You have complete access to your investment.

- With this business, you will have a constant flow of revenue instead of a single income from one sale.

- If you are resourceful enough, you can make a purchase with little money.

- You can retain a house if you are likely to move back in (for instance, if you are being reassigned from a location you are fond of).

- Renting out estates is always lucrative.

- Renting out properties will provide a place for your children to stay, whether now or in the future.

- Purchasing your first property opens the door for you to purchase more.

- Estate price always increases in value.

- You expand your investments.

- There are high benefits when it comes to taxes.

- You can postpone capital profits using a 1031 exchange.

- It can serve as a secondary income.

- It can count as a part of your pension.

- You are able to use your 401k or other pension plans to purchase investment assets.

- It could be a lasting investment.

Disadvantages of Managing Rental Properties

You may likely have moments when you ask yourself why you decided to buy a rental property and become an estate manager. But again, when you plan a review and discover that the value of your estate has appreciated, you'll most likely be happy about the raised profit. In the end, it turns out that the money spent and the time and energy exerted paid off.

However, you must be aware that maintaining rentals has some disadvantages.

- It requires a lot of time investment to start up.

- You have a lot of learning and understanding to do.

- The start-up capital required may be higher than in other investments.

- In the beginning, you may experience low income (deficit financing).

- It can be difficult and time-consuming to stay abreast of technological advancements.

- Accounting for profit and expenditures on your tax return requires added knowledge and time.

- Local, state, and federal laws are countless.

- You will be required to buy more insurance.

- There are risks associated, just like with any other investment.

- You can be indicted.

- You can be manipulated through various means.

- It's not a 9 to 5 job.

- It is similar to having two jobs with no timeout.

- It is no fun when you have to put other things on hold while attending to a crisis.

- It can be difficult to find a freelance construction engineer not to talk about doing business with them.

- It is a public business which means you have to enjoy meeting and talking to people.

- You'll get lots of criticism.

- The market is unstable; always changing.

- Bad situations can happen with renting lands and properties.

Overcoming the Disadvantages

To overcome the difficult aspects of overseeing a rental property, consider these points:

- By now, you already know that getting started is very time-consuming. Keep this in mind and make the time. Knowing how time-consuming this can get and handling things gradually is ultimately helpful.

- Reduce the chances of any likely crisis by devoting your time to the business set up from the get-go and paying attention to details. At the same time, come up with a list of experts whom you are likely to work with and set up appointments with them.

- Keep up to date and simple documentation of all paperwork like receipts and legal documents. Also, seek out software programs that could make documentation easier. If you decide to build your business on a PC, it might save you a lot of energy and time when putting your tax returns in the record. Spend money on a scanner so that all your work can be accessible on the Internet. Invest in a camera, this way you can send the pictures to your PC and upload them on the Internet.

- When you personally oversee the running of your land, your services will be required around the clock and you will have no breaks. Nevertheless, you can make an agreement with associates who also manage their properties on their own to take turns with supervising each other's properties while the other takes a break.

- In some countries, you are not permitted to pay your friends for their services unless they have a legal document, but you have many options. Personally, I know people who live and travel in trailer houses all year, while attending to business through electronic mail and phone calls and gaining access to their finances and documents using the Internet.

- Make inquiries before employing freelance construction workers. In most countries, you must request for legal documents before agreeing to transact business. If this is the case, browse government websites to obtain end-user promotional materials. You are likely to find some helpful information on things to consider before making your choice. Ask your associates (if you have any who manage their own properties) to share some of their contractor's contacts. Also, do not hesitate to ask others how they manage their rental properties. Prepare your mind to hear about their struggles and challenges; do not let them scare you but instead learn from them.

- Have the appropriate amount of insurance and get ready to be litigated, for the just in case. Ensure that you do a yearly assessment of your insurance with your manager. At all times, evaluate your land and properties from a safe and legal perspective.

- Attend training sessions to learn various techniques by which you can address different types of behavioral traits.

- Be a part of the community income landlord association in your neighborhood in order to stay abreast of property-management regulations. Go on the Internet and type in "property owners' association" and your location.

- Keep taking classes and invest your time in reading books.

- Things are bound to take a wrong turn. Anticipate it, and be ready to tackle the problem while being resourceful in your approach.

- Update yourself on the trending technologies.

- Learn to think constructively in times of crisis and stay proactive.

Chapter 2

Making a Business
Out of Rental Properties

Perhaps you've been a real estate manager for a long time, or are just starting up, or you are considering buying your first land, but it is recommended that you think of this as a business. Begin with the fundamentals; make a brand for your business. I recommend you make it simple yet productive in order for you to be able to buy and lease out other lands using that same brand.

Furthermore, you need to decide what you desire to achieve from your new investment (for instance, sole ownership, LLC, trust fund, organization, the list goes on). You can receive legal advice from a lawyer or other experienced landlords.

Your property business requires associating with different experts to gain an understanding of how the business works. Contemplate setting up appointments with asset managers, financial advisors or mortgage brokers, account managers, insurance representatives, and attorneys. Check the segment below for more information. After having decided on what your brand name will be, the type of organization it will become, and consulting with the required experts for knowledge and assistance, you are left with a few other things to be done. This includes:

- **Opening a bank account**: Request that an account be opened in your brand name and make deposit slips having your brand name on them. Doing this buys you a little time at first until you have acquired more assets, and by then it will have saved you a huge amount of time; not to mention that it will make your business more organized. Choose banks with Internet banking options where you can have your money saved in stamps as well as features that allow daily monitoring of your account.

- **Get a Post Office box**: If you wish to maintain your privacy, not desiring for your clients to know your place of residence and you have no office where your clients can post their rent checks, get a second phone number at your home (or a different handset solely for business purposes if you have good reception) and open a Post Office (P.O) box. You may record an informational voice message. Additionally, use your brand name for the e-mail address and not your personal name. When this is completed, put all those details on your business card.

- **Start up a website**: Make it straightforward, nothing complicated - the aim is to have a place on the Internet. Setting one up should be nothing too elaborate and at a reasonable price. You'll be amazed how easy it is to have a site of your own. It will provide potential clients with the necessary details about your estate.

- **Attend classes and training**: Employ experts who will take you through the fundamental things you need to know and also prevent you from making grave mistakes. You can get these through various sources (and allow me to add that this book will help also).

- **Have a plan to keep your assets for an extended period**: You may not always have ownership of land but have arrangements to start building your company from there.

Hiring Real Estate Professionals

A vital thing to consider when you are thinking of buying a landed property or have just begun overseeing your own estate is to organize a functional and effective team to help you make it a success. You are going to have to employ several experts during your venture as well as making their acquaintance- this is to ensure your company's success. Be thorough during the interviews and employ people who can help you build your dreams of becoming a real estate manager. Keep growing and be updated on information in regard to rental properties.

Realtor / Investment banker

The fact that you have a landed property sales permit or that of a landed property broker's permit does not make you a realtor spontaneously. Realtor is the trade name for the National Association of Realtors, and this basically refers to individuals who are authorized by their country to sell landed properties or buildings who also belong to this association.

When you are considering employing someone who will stand in the gap for you when buying your land, employing a realtor is very vital, particularly a realtor who is an expert and knows about the land you are looking to purchase. Consult with other real estate managers that you know if you are having a hard time deciding which realtor to partner with.

Try to form a bond with a realtor on one of your trips to buy landed property, even for the first asset you purchase. You decide what you want when you go in search of properties, despite having a realtor on board. Make findings on your own, browse magazines, newspapers, the Internet. Know what you want and the location you would prefer.

Stockbroker/Investor

An investment banker or insurance broker both help you with anything relating to finance so you can buy a rental property. An investment banker will see to the aspect of helping you get a loan from the bank in which he is employed. An insurance broker, on the other hand, is a freelance agent who works with other banking organizations to help you obtain the best mortgage there is with specifications matching just what you need. Insurance brokers are usually more expensive, by means of what is called points – a charge based on the amount of loan you are receiving.

Provided that you decide to work with a stockbroker, ensure that you set up a meeting with them first before agreeing on prices, this way you can know if you are financially capable, and also know how you will be portrayed on paper to an investor (a procedure known as pre-qualifying). Bear in mind: a lot of investment organizations possess many employees working in the lending unit, as such, it is highly unlikely that you meet with the individual who decides to approve your loan.

Insurance Representative

If you wish to have an effective insurance purchase, you need to have just one go-to agent for all your insurance needs. I recommend forming a business bond with an insurance representative who will oversee all things pertaining to your assets as well as making sure that all your possessions (including your personal residence, your vehicle, etc.) have enough insurance coverage.

Account manager / Financial consultant

It goes without saying that it is vital to set up periodic appointments with your account manager / financial consultant all year round to have discussions concerning your assets and to make an adequate tax record for the year. By doing this, you can discuss everything pertaining to your assets before-hand so that you are well prepared for your meetings with your tax agent, and not be caught off guard by anything when it is time to pay your tax revenue. Some financial consultants have laid-out strategies to help you put your files and documents in order.

You need to have fundamental knowledge of your investments, no doubt; however, nobody expects you to know all the legalities attached to taxes. It is for this reason that you employ an efficient and proactive account manager to deal with your taxes.

Bear in mind that being the owner of real estate has its benefits. You are permitted to remove your buying cost, service expenses, and yearly wear and tear (these benefits do not cease when you employ an expert real estate manager).

Lawyer

I can assure you that you will need a lawyer one day if you own real estate property. You normally want to set up an appointment with a lawyer from the outset to be sure that your business has a sturdy structure and that you have someone you can call when faced with a legal crisis. As a matter of fact, you may want to search for a real estate lawyer whose field of expertise is in the ejection of tenants.

You need to form a business association with a real estate lawyer before being involved in any glitches. You will discover that you can pay for a lawyer's services on an hourly basis depending on how much time was spent during a consultation. If you do proper research, you may discover (for instance) that some lawyers hold a training program nearby or address a group of estate owners. I know that local lawyers in my neighborhood have open discussions at several workshops which I attend. If you can locate and be a part of a neighboring landlord gathering, I can almost assure you that they will arrange for a lawyer to address you at least once a year.

Estate manager

An estate manager is an expert who specializes in overseeing investment properties (lands and buildings), on behalf of others; most of the time, what he/she does is oversees the running of the property and takes care of rental. The mere fact that someone is a realtor does not make them qualified to oversee your properties. Browse on National Association of Residential Property Managers at www.NARPM.org, or check the Institute of Real Estate Managers at www.IREM.org. There you will be provided with a number of professional estate managers who abide by an ethical code. Pick out those who have invested in securing a license for themselves and/or for their organizations.

Although you may make up your mind to oversee your property by yourself, I would still recommend that you acquaint yourself with a local estate manager in your neighborhood.

Stretching Yourself To Take That Step

The money aspect of your recent buy can seem like complicated and befuddling bookkeeping. I'll tell you upfront that there is a lot to know in this department, so don't strain yourself in trying to figure it out alone. This is what your financial manager is there for. Always bear in mind that the options are inexhaustible, so do your research! Furthermore, discover whether your town, state, or district offers any housing programs that can benefit you financially, either in buying or remodeling your property.

Majority of prosperous financiers have a history of expanding themselves to move into their first property. Most real estate moguls can also relate to you how they bought their initial property as well as how they started the business. In any case, starting up and making the first move is the most difficult and the most terrifying part of all measures.

Don't have the notion that you have to "start big" and begin with large properties. Your starting point can be as simple as buying a second house and rent out the one in which you live presently. If you have yet to buy any properties at all, consider investing in a two or three story building and live in one of the units. By doing so, you get tax write-offs and build equity. You can start with renovations on the property while and at the same time as building equity the value appreciates.

Chapter 3

More Financing Options

Throughout this book, I make references to managing your landed properties as a "business investment." The surest way of keeping things in the right perspective is by doing this, especially when it comes to satisfying local, state, and federal requirements and responsibilities; accounting for money transactions as well as paying necessary charges. If you designed your investment property to be a big business, it will help you stay on the line of your goal as you advance and acquire more investment properties.

You must be able to account for how much money is coming in and how much you are spending for the sake of state and federal taxes, as well as to help you keep proper records. Subtract your expenditures from the amount of money coming in to help you know whether you are making money on the business or running a loss, as well as to help you calculate the amount you will pay as tax. Bear in mind that being an owner of real estate comes with its benefits and tax remuneration. Some of the many benefits you can enjoy includes being able to remove the total service expenses and decrease in value from your total income as the investment worth continues to increase in value as time passes.

Having said that, the legalities associated with taxes for a rental property are usually more complicated than those required for an individual dwelling. The laws guiding taxes are not different and they are not stable, which makes it challenging to stay updated. Because of this, a vital aspect of owning real estate is having a certified public accountant (CPA) as well as a qualified financial organizer who has a remarkable understanding of property management.

Something else you need to have is a vast knowledge about taxes and everything that is required of you, at the same time, be informed about various obtainable insurance packages to help bail you out of any crisis. Furthermore, you must be aware of the local government agencies around you and do well to oblige to all requirements. License and yearly assessments by the fire department and state inspection officers are obligatory in some states or countries to ensure security and wellbeing.

Income can be broadly classified into two in the tax work namely: ordinary revenue and capital profits. Ordinary revenue encompasses your take-home pay, remuneration, additional benefits, bonuses, rental income, and interest revenue. Taxes are removed at differing tariffs based on your tax bracket.

In contrast, capital profits require more skillfulness. It is a tax generated from the money you gain when you sell your stock and investment properties. There is a modus operandi for everything; your ordinary income and your capital gains income. You must keep proper documentation and make sure it is well arranged; this way you'll have everything prepared for when you meet up with your account manager. Have a good forecast and be ready for anything. Manage your taxes well so you'll know when you need to sell a property and when to enlarge it.

Types of Taxes

Taxes are of various forms including state taxes, federal taxes, and local taxes. In some locations, there are county taxes, real estate taxes, and the exquisite company taxes. See your account manager for more information. Also, check with your account manager for an explicit explanation, and make certain that you are keeping with every requirement.

State tax: There are states that lack state taxes; this is interpreted as you not needing to do a state tax return. Meet up with the state government of where your property is located and request for details concerning taxes. It is likely that your account manager has an office in that state, and knows someone there who they can get you in contact with to get trending information. Several states have a transfer tax or a revenue tax, all of which makes a bulk of property management taxes. If you are in a state that uses this form of taxation, after you might have done a tax return, your account manager may then help you to prepare a document that shows the gross and net income produced from your investment properties and estimate the outstanding.

In some states, a permit fee for landlords is made compulsory. An example of this is yearly dues for a business permit depending on the size of your estate or how much you make from it. The permit fee may also be deemed mandatory for rental properties. Nevertheless, taxes come most frequently as a percentage of the — total money coming in (gross income), and not after removing the expenditure (net income) — money generated by you.

Federal tax: Federal (National) tax concerns everyone. Your federal tax return should be documented by you yearly. Also, you are expected to have a concise record of the income generated from your asset as well as your expenditures. You may likely pay your tax based on your net income and this may vary from what your colleague is paying, as determined by your company's structure (see Chapter 1), as well as the way you manage your asset.

Organizing your estate can be done in various ways. Anyone of these can be your pick: organization, partnership, and LLC. A competent account manager will give counsel on your current circumstances. For instance, if your rental property is managed like a corporation, he/she may recommend that you remove all revenue from your account by the end of the year to prevent a high corporate tax. You wouldn't like for your organization to be taxed twice. Remove the money from your account and tag it as revenue, then use it for upgrading your estate or to settle debts. Your account manager has knowledge of what is excellent for your business in this regard.

Asset tax: Asset (property) tax is often ad valorem (obligatory at the percentage worth) which a property owner pays based on the worth of the land. A few state taxes are determinant of the magnitude and utility of the land. The tax agency carries out or requests the land evaluation to know the worth of the estate or land, and the tax is reviewed based on that worth.

The key segment of most local government administration collects the largest percentage of service funds through taxes generated from estate and property management within their community. In many situations, asset tax goes up on a regular basis through different evaluations based on expansion, voted-in measures, schools, or urgent situations. These costs may either be percentage based or fixed rates, as determined by the public or legal representatives.

The land or building is often evaluated by an expert when you buy the land. By doing so, they can decide on the worth of the land and other similar properties in that location. Coming up with a reasonable selling price of a real estate involves three techniques, namely: comparing sales, the cost method, and the income method. Evaluators and tax appraisers often make use of more than one of the methods stated above to ensure accuracy in the concluding estimation.

Know that lands and houses are evaluated individually. Almost every country has a laid out structure of how an estate or land is re-evaluated or reviewed from time to time. Hence, the greater value placed on your property, the greater the tax. Most countries have their property taxes paid twice annually.

Property tax is a massive, flat expenditure. Although taxes are not paid on a monthly basis, you must still estimate their cost when drawing your monthly financial plan. Some landlords include taxes and insurance fee in their monthly mortgage. This practice is referred to as escrow account / impound account, and it is to make certain that you can raise this huge amount of money required twice a year. Always pay up your property tax when it is due to avoid paying a fine (which is usually around 10%). In many countries, you are permitted to make installment payments using your credit cards without extra charges, and perhaps your credit card stores points or airline mileage on every charge you make, your points will accumulate fast enough if you make your tax payment this way.

Several creditors deal with non-payment of tax within the mortgage formalities and can call back your loan, ensuring that you pay it back right away if you have refused a tax payment.

Individual property tax is also required in some states. Hence, if you have put a fridge, washing machine/dryer, or other furnishings and fittings in the house, you will be required to document these as well. Most times, the most efficient way to go about this is by getting in touch with the state government or district agent for the complete list of taxes that they require or you could sort this matter out with your account manager.

Transfer tax: This tax is usually charged when the land or building is being sold. Normally, it is charged by the state at no stable rate but varies from location to location. This charge is mostly deducted during the escrow process of buying or selling land or a building.

Value Depreciation

While estimating your annual tax revenue, the state or federal administration permits the owners of rental properties to remove the reduction value. Note that reduction value is not an out-of-pocket expenditure you laid on yourself. Instead, it is an accounting theory which permits you to subtract natural depreciation as well as protect your revenue. This is intended not just to help with natural depreciation, but in addition, afford you additional money flow. Also, it has nothing to do with your building's appearance of deterioration.

Maintenance vs. repair: The general law is that the money spent on repairs can be removed from the tax in the year that it is used. Maintenance, on the other hand, is distributed over time. This means that larger sums should be deducted over time while lesser ones can be completely removed from the tax returns the same year it is spent.

Active vs. passive: It is vital to know how it varies from the IRS perspective and for the purpose of taxes. If you are involved in rental property and sales, and this is your main line of business, there are no limits to the losses of dollar value if you can own and harness against your income.

To most people, real estate is a second career. If this is the case with you, IRS has a restriction of $25,000 on yearly loss removal. Broadly speaking, you are an inactive (passive) financier if you are what some describe as a silent associate. As a passive financier, you can use wear and tear deduction to equalize every revenue from your asset.

By IRS criteria, you have an active role in every decision involving your rental property, irrespective of whether you have an expert management organization in position. You are regarded as an active financier if you contribute to major decisions like, choice of tenants, rental price, or main renovations.

There are several resourceful methods by which you can obtain all the benefits as well as obtain complete write-offs through your accountant's expertise.

Building Permits and Licenses

The city government is well known for charging building permit fees. The basis of this tax is on the proportion of the overall development cost of a recent structure.

Business licenses are starting to be routine qualifications for rental properties. A business license is mandatory for each property owned in several counties and cities. What is calculated is the number of units and the profit generated, and you are charged on a percentage or a flat rate per unit. This amount is typically due yearly. To know the amount you are to pay, ask your county offices or local city.

Insurance

Rented out properties require a landlord's insurance policy. Despite your home being in the same building, plain landlord's insurance policy does not include rental property most times. As a homeowner, you have invested substantially in the property you rent out and you have minimal power over the physical damage that can befall it. You should have excellent insurance for your rental property which includes vandalism liability, preservation from fire, and other physical losses that can occur. Aside having insurance against physical losses, insurance is also needed in cases of lawsuits to protect you and your assets.

Keep in mind that there are many types of insurance coverages made available by various insurance carriers. Look around for these different options or better yet hire an insurance agent to do the work for you. The insurance agent should carefully describe the coverage and explain in detail the cons and pros.

Types of Insurance

Obtaining good insurance is as crucial as obtaining a good loan: you require a suitable coverage for condition, and this is what a good insurance agent can help you determine. When you make a decision on the coverage that gives you satisfaction and is in line with what your lender requires, look around again and make comparisons with other forms of insurance coverages.

- **Fire and liability**: Having both fire and liability insurance is a requirement by lenders as this serves as a security guarantee. This insurance serves as a protection to you and your lender from unplanned accidents. A fire, no matter how small, is costly and you want to be able to repair and reconstruct your property to what it was like initially as much as possible. Ensure you have liability coverage and replacement coverage. Fire and liability insurance is not an option, it is a necessity.

- **Umbrella Coverage**: Some refer to it as "blanket coverage." It acts as a supplement to other insurance plans and an economical method to reduce risk. The umbrella coverage serves as a backup if you are involved in a huge lawsuit that your other insurance plan cannot cover. For condominium owners, who are not covered by standard fire insurance, umbrella coverage can be used. In events like this, protect yourself from liability even if the landlord's union covers fire insurance.

- **Flood Insurance**: This form of insurance is required more than you think. It is referred to as a rider policy, hence sold separately from your other insurance policies. Before purchasing your property, ask if it is located in a flood plain. This information is provided at the time of purchase and if it is confirmed that the property is in a flood plain, most lenders will require flood insurance.

- **Natural Disaster Insurance**: Insurance for natural disasters like earthquakes, hurricanes, winds, and hail are sold separately as a rider to your present policy. This insurance is totally optional as it is not needed in all areas. Insurance for an earthquake is very costly and it is known to have a very huge deductible.

- **Mortgage Insurance**: In cases such as disability or death, when you cannot pay off your mortgage, this insurance pays the remainder.

- **Workers Compensation**: If you have employees, temporary or permanent, this insurance is a necessity. This insurance protects you from liability such as paying medical bills or loss of wages from accidents that can occur in the process of carrying out duties like maintenance or professional duties connected to your company. You may feel like you have no employees but the law says you do. That onsite foreman and every other worker you have on the rental property are covered by this policy. An employee is simply someone who receives payment for services provided, so the uninsured and unauthorized artisan or friend are all covered. If you are employing an authorized artisan, confirm that they have their own workers' compensation policies.

- **Non-Owner Auto Liability**: This form of insurance is not costly and covers employees that drive for you. Liabilities for accidents and injuries that can occur when your driver is using his/her own vehicles are covered by this policy.

- **Building Ordinance Coverage**: It is a relevant insurance coverage in that it protects you in case of destruction (complete or partial) of your rental property. It covers the cost of everything required to rebuild including demolition, cleanup, and cost of ensuring the building meets the new building requirements which might turn out to be more strict.

- **Tenant's Insurance**: Since your insurance does not cover your tenant's personal possessions, it is best to encourage them to get their own insurance. Hence, tenant's insurance is basically the insurance that the tenant pays for. It is of great significance that your tenants are aware of the fact that their personal possessions are not covered by your (landlord's) insurance. In the event of theft, fire, water damage, and any other kind of loss that can happen to a tenant's personal possessions, tenant's insurance covers the losses. Encourage your tenants to get their own insurance.

- **Home Warranty Insurance**: Depending on the systems in your home, home warranty insurance covers the deterioration or failures of the different systems in your house such as plumbing, furnace (depending on the age of your home), garage doors, electrical appliances, etc. Items such as the furnace incur a large amount when fixing them so having a home warranty insurance reduces the expenses. Homes bought in the last five years might not need this, as it is dependent on the age of your home.

Reducing Risks Through Preventive Maintenance

You do not have to wait for unfortunate situations or a lawsuit before taking measures to prevent them. Imbibe a preventive mindset, don't wait for things to get worse before doing anything: assess your property for problems, check the lights, and check the sidewalk for any tripping hazards. Look around for hazardous materials or conditions that can bring about lawsuits and ensure that they do not become risks. Prevention is cheaper than complete repairs.

Ensure the safety of your property, and escape the pain of going through lawsuits.

Reviewing Your Policy

Find time to reevaluate your insurance plan with your agent, instead of just paying your insurance yearly. Ask your insurance agent to look for better carriers, if you employed an agent. Aim to reevaluate your insurance plan at the same time annually. For instance, I see my insurance agent every March, we meet at my office, and I make sure we reevaluate every single aspect of every policy. By the time you realize what's going on, you'll discover that you are underinsured, and your present insurance coverage is not suitable for the present day's value. Guard your investment with as much insurance as you can get.

A very necessary aspect of owning a rental property is having great insurance coverage.

Chapter 4

Owning a Rental Property

People become landlords and start a renting business for various reasons, and these reasons are not far-fetched. Some start with the hope of property appreciation (which is the increase in the value of the property through the period in which you are the owner) and good income, and are well aware of the huge amount of work that needs to be put forth.

Some find themselves in that position and did not choose to own a rental property. At times, it is due to a relocation from the area for their jobs or they decide to take a leave which can last for about a year or two. In these cases, they do not sell their homes because they plan to come back. Hence, the home was not designed to be a rental property, but they found out that getting returns from it pays their bills. Other cases includes parents getting older coupled with the need to start residing in an assisted living facility. The property can be kept as a legacy and it is rented out to pay the costs of living at the dwelling.

Acquiring a Rental Property

Some of the ways you can convert your present home to a rental property are discussed in this aspect.

Temporary assignment / job transfer: The nature of some jobs, especially that of a professional or an executive, can require a short-term transfer to another country or city from where their home is located for a period of time. The best way to go is highly dependent on the specific situation you find yourself in. You will need to consider employing a professional property management company if you will be going out of the state or country.

Moving to a nursing home: As parents grow older, they might have to relocate to a rest home or an assisted living facility. Some of the options available are to rent out the home to help with expenditure and evade tax liabilities. Make sure you speak to a professional to understand the significance of whatever decision you make. Retaining the home is also a way of keeping a legacy and it serves as a source of funding for emergency cases whose cost are not included in other categories.

Death of a parent: The death of a parent is a very emotional event, especially if you were living together, and this will require more time to think about and reflect on what the best option is moving forward. In this case, you follow the same steps as moving your parents to an assisted living facility, only this time you take your time doing it. Spending more time before doing this can also aid healing.

Don't forget that death occurring in a home is a piece of information that must be disclosed to a potential tenant.

The property you have been trying to sell: Contemplate renting out your home if you've been trying to sell it and it's still on the market and you are dedicated to getting new property. At times, you might enjoy having your first home as a rental but the market can change in a year or so. Ensure that you discuss with your financial planner and/or accountant to be sure you are making the best decision at that time. You are better off renting your property if you deduce that you will incur losses in selling. If the property is sold when the market is down, the loss incurred will be less.

Purchase an investment property: Purchasing an investment property can be a good decision for your financial portfolio when interest rates are low and the stock market is unstable. Before closing the purchase, some very important factors should be considered. "Location, location, location" is a mantra that pertains to your rental units as much as it's applicable to your home.

Compare property values and rent: Firstly, carry out thorough background research. Make a decision on which area you want to make a purchase. If you can, talk to your friends about their investments, the places they own properties, and the state of affairs in that location. When you've made a decision on the area, city, or country you would like to make a purchase, make a bid before entering a contract, ensure you appraise the area's property values, and study them in contrast to the property you want to purchase. Study both property values and compare with other rentals in the area. Ask questions if the rent is very low, and if you notice any unclear numbers or huge differences.

You should make inquiries at your city's planning department or the Chamber of Commerce to know if there will be large scale adjustments on the properties in the area in the future. Take for instance a major freeway being built, just a block away, a month after purchasing your property.

Explore different loan alternatives: Inspect all loans properly to see what their outcome will be like in a few years. The property can go from a good investment to a bad one if one takes an adjustable rate loan and the interest hits the roof. Most investors prefer interest-only loans to increase their profit on investment. Stay sensible, you do not know what may come up in the future.

Take property tax into consideration: Investors mostly make their purchases in accordance with the existing property tax laws. Once the investors buy a property at a higher value, the taxes on the property then increase. This trap should be avoided at all cost. You are to research on the state's tax laws as well as the tax changes likely to occur and then include the estimated tax into your calculations.

Consider supplemental tax: There are states that hold you accountable for the payment of supplemental tax. The supplemental tax should be paid to the tax assessor of that state as it is a local tax. The money to be paid is a percent of what the cost of the property was given by the previous owners and is then compared to how much you purchased it for.

Look into insurance coverage: Insurance can also be increased like a tax bill. You will also want to add a policy of the "landlord/rental" into the amount estimated in order to get more security than the usual homeowner's insurance policy. Although a lot of states have been subjected to natural disasters, leading to the rise in insurance policies, it is not a cause for alarm as most landlords' policies are within a fair range.

Ensure that you find out if there had been any insurance claims on the property in the past three years and if you can obtain insurance before buying the property.

Confirm the costs of utility: Companies providing utilities such as sewer, water, and garbage locally should be checked in order to find out if they will send bills to the tenant. Utilities provided in common areas such as lighting, water heater, sprinklers, swimming pool, air conditioning, outside lights, as well as the laundry room would also be paid for and should be included in your estimates.

Plan for possible maintenance costs: The money spent on the maintenance of a property depends on the property purchased. Practical estimates are needed to be obtained if you happen to buy a property needing repairs. Buying a property of high quality does not excuse planning for its maintenance. Your home should be used as an example, as you reflect on your efforts in maintaining it. There is always room for improvement.

Consultation with your real estate agent and financial planner: Your financial plans could change due to the changes in tax laws. Ensure that you seek advice from people who are experienced in property finances. Do not forget that selection of the right property with appropriate financing will ensure that the changes in tax laws will not affect you.

Inspection of the property: Thorough examination of the property should be done before purchasing it. In the event that you cannot do the inspection personally, ensure you get someone you trust to carry it out for you. An experienced inspector should be employed in order to carefully inspect the design and construction of the property so as to achieve a secure investment. Ensure you get the appropriate information before committing in the long run and getting a long-term loan.

Also, while examining the property, you are to seek the expertise of a contractor as well as the pest control of the property, the engineer's statements, the pool, the roof, survey and chimneys should all be taken into consideration while examining the property. These reports, though expensive and time-consuming, help in keeping your investments safe and secure for the long run.

Transforming Your Property Into a Rental

It is impossible for all properties to make good rentals as some have better standards than others. Ensure that practical and financial decisions be implemented even though all properties are rented at a price with a level of risk. Here are a number of properties that may not be suitable for rent:

Homes sited at poor locations: Location of a home is critical. Homes that make good rentals are sited in a good neighborhood, close to shopping areas, work sites, public transportation, and in a great school district. They should typically not be located beside a shopping center, school, or on busy streets; neither should they be located up a long winding road or far out in the country as tenants may not like the stress accompanied with the long drive to get to their homes. Although they may be cheaper to purchase, the amount you receive from the rent would also be cheap.

It is important to seriously think about the location when buying any property. Good neighborhoods attract good tenants.

A house with a pool: Although most people believe that a house with a pool is an asset and makes the rental more suitable, this is not always true. This is because a pool is just another item of worry and could be more of a liability. People may not want a pool due to the maintenance cost, the likelihood of an accident occurring in or out of the pool, and also the correct operation of the pump.

When you have a pool, you are to add the amount of the pool service in the monthly rent. Do not forget that having a pool increases the monthly expenses and insurance rates.

An old-fashioned home: Newer houses rarely have issues with their upkeep and maintenance while problems may arise from dealing with outdated homes. Maintenance issues which could either be major or minor are the characteristics of older homes. The moment a major appliance stops working, the tenant will want it fixed post-haste. You are to make sure that the property is comfortable and safe and should also be up to the standards of public health and safety, before putting it on the market for rent.

Homes that are high-maintenance: When you have your own home, you should be willing to and may even like performing chores such as cutting and watering the lawn, watering the flowers, fixing things, and raking fallen leaves around the property. It is almost a guarantee that your tenants would not give as much care to the property. They may speak about how much they would wish to, but would never find the time to do so.

The property should consist of drip systems for irrigation timed to work at various intervals. A gardener should also be employed and paid monthly with the expense added to the rent of the tenant. You should be familiar with the cost of maintaining a property with multiple apartments or units with a yard or larger land area.

Purchasing An Occupied Rental Property

The rental property you are about to buy may already have been rented out to tenants. It is important to know the procedures to ensure that no problems arise during the handing over from the previous owner to you, the current owner. Here is a list of things that need to be read, revised, signed, and compared with the lease contract when purchasing a property already in use by a tenant:

i.   A current copy of the insurance policy.

ii.   The previous rental contract as well as other contracts that were signed afterward.

iii.   A comprehensive list of all personal items added in the sale.

iv.   The paperwork used for screening as well as rental applications for all adult tenants living in the property.

v.   Copy of present vacant units and current rent roll.

vi.   The copies of the reports on the condition of the property before the tenant moved in.

vii.   A copy of the property's tax bill.

viii. The contacts of the tenants such as phone numbers and e-mail addresses.

ix. Copies of any type of special or business license needed for the property.

x. The keys to all doors, rooms, gates, and storage units.

xi. Statements of the money earned and spent in the last six months or one year should be included.

xii. Copies of the letters indicating an increase in the rent of the tenant.

xiii. Copies of bills paid on utility as well as any invoices.

xiv. Requests for maintenance as well as correspondence should be collected from the previous owner.

xv. The copies of all written contracts.

xvi. A record of payments from the existing owner.

xvii. In order to help understand the contracts with the maintenance companies, previous contract copies should be received in advance.

xviii. Copies of notices given to the tenant including proof-of-service notice should be included.

xix. The total security deposits paid by the tenant to the owner at the end of escrow.

xx. An affidavit, known as Estoppel certificates, received from the tenants showing how much rent they pay, the deposit paid when they moved in, and other things they would like to address.

xxi. Copies of the property's plans and diagrams, particularly for during emergencies, showing where the light timers, large appliance shut-off valves, and water-timers are located.

xxii. Paint brand and colors used in painting the interior and exterior of the property by former owners.

This list of items is to be received before the end of escrow. It is advisable to present a comprehensive list to your realtor so he or she can allow the present owner to collect and make required copies at the expected time.

Closing on the loan and meeting your tenants: There are some things you need to do once you are the new owner following the end of escrow. You are to contact your tenants sending them an official letter informing them that you are the current owner. You will also need to inform them of the new address they are to mail their rent payments to. The previous owner should also write a letter of introduction in order to avoid the problem of where and whom the rent is to be paid. You can also visit your tenants personally if you wish to.

When going to the property, ensure that you take along the letter of introduction from the previous owner as well as your contact information. You are to go through the property with your tenants and be mindful that your tenants will ask for various things pertaining to the property. Inform them of your plans, which could include reviewing the cost of rent in relation to the market, sending them new rental contracts, or serve them advance notification to vacate the property. Ensure to check out the rental control laws if available.

Hiring a realtor: A realtor is a member of the National Association of Realtors (NAR). They are to guide themselves in accordance to the Realtor's Code of Ethics and must abide by the rules and regulations of the professional association. They must be authorized by the state and work for a licensed real estate broker. I recommend that you hire a professional realtor. You can bluntly ask questions such as, "Are you a licensed realtor, on the local board, or are you a member of the National Association of Realtors?"

Hiring a professional real estate agent should be done with as much care as you would with a doctor or lawyer. You can get good referrals from friends, neighbors, and co-workers. Ensure to inquire as much as possible about their home buying as well as selling experiences, if they would choose to work with this particular agent again, the kind of services they received and if they would work with a particular real estate brokerage company once again.

Purchasing an investment property is a huge task and can include financial and legal problems. A realtor is someone who specializes in attending to all facets of the transactions, and his or her experience as a professional works as an advantage for the party (buyer or seller) he or she represents. You feel secure hiring a realtor knowing that your real estate transactions are following the due process because a trained professional, who can foresee problems that are likely to arise, can offer possible solutions suited for such problems.

Hiring a Real Estate Agent

A real estate agent is an important person to obtain. You will most likely require someone to watch out for the appropriate property for you to buy, as well as be your representative during the purchase process. Therefore, you need the expertise of a professional who is licensed as a real estate agent. This person is a vital part of the process of buying a rental property. There are usually lots of real estate agents in a given area to choose from; you need to know how to go about hiring the right person suited for you.

Agent, subagent, and listing agent: A subagent is a dual agent, unlike the listing agent who acts as the representative of the owner of the property and is different from a buyer's agent who represents the buyer alone.

Talking to real estate agents who are experienced in the selling and purchasing of properties, which are investment-types, can help you get ideas about the business. You can find them by going through the real estate advertisements in your local newspaper. Check out those with rental property listings put up for sale, despite the fact that you have no interest in the property. You are to focus on the real estate companies, particularly those in your locality. Realtors working in your area will be able to answer questions about issues of interest such as taxes, businesses, and schools, as they will be better equipped in selecting the best location.

Collect a referral of the professional property manager from whom you can obtain the information needed on rental values and what to look for when purchasing an investment property in that area from your realtor.

More importantly, ensure that you are at ease with the realtor you choose because developing trust is an important factor.

Chapter 5

Financing Rental Property

Starter real estate investors may encounter different problems while purchasing rental properties. The two situations here are to be able to discover the perfect investment property in the most appropriate location and to ponder about a budget and a financial strategy to incorporate. Essentially, this is the source your real estate investment property depends on. Actually, financial rental properties shouldn't be a problem in any way.

Having a wide idea for financial rental property options is the healthiest way to begin. That is, if you have acquired a better knowledge of your choices, endeavor to begin saving and planning for financial rental properties with minimal problems.

Conventional Bank Loans

This is a type of loan made available to you via private granters like banks, credit unions, or mortgage companies. What are the requirements before the approval for this type of loan? Actually, the granter or lender will be concerned about your credit score together with credit history. Apart from getting approval, much relies on how genuine you have been actively borrowing and paying debts incurred in the past. That is, the monthly mortgage payments, the time to pay, and also the interest rates involved.

Granters or lenders will surely go through your current income, your assets, and also ascertain your latest mortgage. The idea is to know whether you have the cash flow that will be able to pay for financial rental properties, which will only include your current remuneration. There is no way you can add other potential rental income from positive cash flow in which you know that the rental property will affect you.

Being a starter in real estate investment, you should know that this type of loan will involve an advance payment. Some granters may ask for 20%, while others might require as high as 30%, because investment properties are seen as a risk. Note, before you request for this type of loan, draft out a budget plan for your personal finances and save the cash, in order to make financing rental properties efficient and effective down the line.

Residential Loan (for one to four units)

There are various options available to choose from; all the more if you're thinking of staying in the property or owner-occupied, as the granters call it. In a case where the property is an owner-occupied property, then the granter often requests 3% to 20% down. In a nutshell, this means that you will provide 20% or let the current owner take back 10% to stand as a second mortgage. It is advisable to investigate with the granter you chose to work with concerning their granting policy to know whether a second loan can be available. This is because many granters don't give the opportunity for a second loan. Don't be limited by fears to approach two or three lenders with the same loan idea, as it will help present you with more choices or options.

When one granter disagrees, you can receive approval from another. Try using your real estate property-management professional to get a referral to a loan broker who could help you and move along the process.

However, there are times you may find a lender desiring to offer a 95% loan solely on an owner-occupied property. Moreover, placing the least and holding enough cash on hand is the ideal way to go. In case something shows up during your establishment, or better yet, when an opportunity presents itself to acquire an available investment property, you should go for it. When you have a loan ranging above 80%, then you may be requested to own private mortgage insurance, also considered in the business as PMI. This is insurance protection set aside for the lender against repossession. Other added costs are made available when you're requested to have PMI, which often comes with a more increase in interest rate. Also, you may be levied higher points in order to conceal the cost of the insurance.

The point here is that the granter levies on top of other payments, which is equal to 1% of your loan amount. Meaning when a granter charges you $100,000 loan amount for 2 points, it amounts to $2,000. There are other costs you still have related to the loan, such as the appraisal fees, lender fees, and title insurance costs. All these can easily sum up to a high amount of money.

Government Programs

The Federal Housing Administration (FHA) came into existence to promote homeownership. There are various ways it encourages homebuyers, including giving them the opportunity to purchase property having just 3.5% down. Irrespective of the fact that FHA loans are distinctively planned to further the buying of owner-occupied homes, it gives the chance to purchase a two, three and even four-unit building, in which you can live in one unit, and procure income from the others. Realistically, this is a wonderful cost-effective means to fund a rental property, particularly if it's your first.

These FHA loan limits differ from one area to another, ensuring that the loan limit at the place you desire to buy is high enough to enable you to buy a multi-unit property.

Fix-and-flip Loans

Are you thinking of being a landlord and also renting to tenants? However, if your purpose is to invest in a house in order to fix it, and bring it back to the market, then a distinctive loan is available that you should be notified of: the fix-and-flip loan. To be eligible for this loan, you don't need to be as credit-worthy as with a typical bank loan. While granters will go through your credit history and income, the loan focuses mainly on the worth of the investment property on its own. Considering the after-repair-value of the rental property, granters will decide if you will be capable to offer the mortgage payments.

Nevertheless, you could qualify for financial rental properties within a few days if the perfect investment property idea is adopted. There's an investment property calculator available you can use to help you ascertain the worth of an investment property before you bid for this type of loan.

There are some negative points to a fix-and-flip loan. Part of it is that it's short term, most times less than one year. Also, the interest rates happen to be higher than with conventional loans, together with the origination fees and closing costs. Besides, if you are wishing to gain very fast from an investment property, rather than rely on monthly rental income, then this could be the perfect real estate investing course for you.

Home Equity

Even if you're a starter real estate investor, do you have a home already? If you do, you could borrow in contrary to the equity of that home. Most lenders will give you the opportunity to borrow nearly 80% of home equity to fund rental properties. Three kinds of loans are available for home equity.

- **Home Equity Loan**: To be eligible, granters have to ensure you're capable to pay back by assessing and analyzing your income and credit history. They will check your mortgage for the house along with the worth of your home.

    If you qualify, it's possible there's cash you can get up front. Going from there, it functions the same way as a conventional bank loan, where you will possess an established monthly payment which is generally interest only, though the rate could be variable. Loans of this type often have a lengthy payment time, such as 15-20 years.

- **Home Equity Line of Credit (HELOC)**: Although home equity loans are indistinguishable to conventional loans, HELOC are akin to a credit card. You'll get a credit amount you can borrow from or charge to. HELOC will aid you in paying monthly with interest. Eligibility for this line of credit needs the exact requirements as a home equity loan.

- **Cash-Out Refinance**: This path demands the same steps of application and qualification just like a conventional bank loan. That is, a cash-out refinance stands to pay the available debt you owe on your present property, giving way for another mortgage to be created. Cash-out here, is paid to you as the difference. It has an agreed rate, but you could at the end of the day pay more in interest over your real mortgage.

Seller Financing

Most real estate investors are busy funding rental properties via seller financing. Options like this are taken when you're not eligible for conventional loans. The plan here means the seller of the house specifically takes the position of the bank. If you take over the ownership, you'll be responsible to pay monthly installments to the seller of the property.

The property seller will be glad to tread your path if you have a well financed idea set forth coupled with investment strategies for effective cash-flow. Failing to follow the agreement, the seller of the property can take back the house, just like a bank can do if you fail to pay off your mortgage loans.

Teaming Up

Be it that you're looking for just one original estate colleague or seeking for a handful of investors to come together, several investors funding rental properties combined is an alternative. Like this, if you own an average or a third of the investment, you can overlook the loans from banks waiting to be approved. Also, you can purchase the investment property and begin gaining from that moment. Purchasing rental properties involves many risks, and not everything will rely on you. Be cautious when selecting your real estate colleague. Let it be someone you can depend on, a person you reason similarly with in areas of a real estate investment strategy and a financial idea. Secure a real estate lawyer to prepare any necessary legal documents and ensure you don't crash into any of the tricks of real estate partnerships.

Retirement Accounts

Most people who have developed jobs consistently or have worked for themselves for years possess retirement money in an IRA. When you own an IRA that could direct itself, you're free to invest in unconventional assets, that is, in something other than stocks or mutual funds. Real estate is an agreed investment class, which means that money can be used in a self-directed IRA to fund a rental property.

If you follow this, try to first notify your CPA. With the availability of software that makes it simpler to become a landlord, real estate is more of a practical investment than anything else in the stock market. Before you rush into it, ensure you're prepared to invest the time and power required to see a valuable return on investment.

Real Estate Crowdfunding

This is a relatively recent idea that presents itself with a social network for funding rental properties. What real estate crowdfunding basically does is to manipulate the power of social media networks in order to promote investment opportunities. There are not many real estate crowdfunding programs that you can consult, and every one of them has its own rules and regulations of how it operates. Basically, at the point of investing in real estate via crowdfunding, there's a loan you would be taking in which will be funded by the investors of the program. Optionally, investors collect a section of the equity on the investment property. Hence, you'll need to hand-over a return on investment to them whether you sell or take from the positive cash flow in rental income.

Being a new real estate investor, this idea for funding rental properties is not the perfect plan, because real estate crowdfunding involves many requirements to qualify, together with a past of good investment choices. Though, it's a choice you shouldn't forget easily while building your real estate investment profile and desire different ways to fund investments.

Don't Forget Details Matter

Irrespective of how you fund your rental property, ensure you have enough paperwork at hand to effectively help you reach success and gain frequent income from the property you purchase. This means investing in the following:

- Conventionally written agreements involving a seller who has accepted to lend you money for property buying.

- Legitimate documentation, such as an LLC operating agreement, to clarify the positions of people and the remuneration in a partnership.

- The estimation of expected returns coming from different kinds of investment from your financial planner to enable you to balance potential outcomes.

Investing in real estate can be beneficial and productive as well. In order to enjoy its advantages, endeavor to protect the details from the outset.

Funding rental properties shouldn't be a problem, as there are many choices to think about. When you fully understand your choices, you'll be able to equip yourself for the future in order to help you qualify easily for the funding. The fact that you may not have a lot of money doesn't mean that you can't begin investing in real estate.

Chapter 6

Managing The Cash Flow

The income from the real estate business has aided some of the most opulent people in the world in amassing wealth. Even though the majority started as proprietors of smaller multi-unit buildings, they soon expanded to dealing in bigger commercial properties. It is arguable to say that in real estate, earning passive income is the only thing that investors strive for.

In the real estate industry, there are endless means of generating capital; therefore an investor must appreciate the benefits of understanding the cash flow of the industry in order to seize arising opportunities for the most gain. Of these endless means, a very typical example is rental properties.

Cash Flow

Cash flow is the number of earnings an investor has after having paid their total bill; it's how much the investor will most likely take home in the end. This money embodies gains later used for reinvestment in other events or saving for retirement. Succinctly put, cash flow exemplifies an equitable amount of surplus money after accounting for every capital expense made by the investor.

More often than not, investors use estimates from cash flow summations to ascertain the benefits of investing in a particular property. If you are contemplating venturing into rental properties, understanding how cash flow is actuated and knowing the expenses to account for should be a priority.

How to Determine the Cash Flow

It is less difficult for experienced investors to unearth the real potential of a rental. However, the estimation of cash flow is as easy as deducting all expenses from your total income, thus, mastery is not particularly required, and neither do you need to be a professional before you can sum rental cash flow by yourself. The procedure is somewhat easy provided you have all the important details. Seeing that income and expenses are best described as mere vague notions, below is a more elaborate breakdown on how to estimate the cash flow capacity of a property.

Summation of the income: You can begin by establishing the expected earnings in the rental estate over a period of one year. Thoroughly ascertain what is referred to as *local comps* (comparable properties) in your market and find out the probable amount that the property can be rented out per month. Comps are the most preferred method of estimating the rental income amount in a particular region, provided the comps are done accurately. You can try talking to realtors in that area or to companies that are into the supervision of properties in order to assess the rent of your chosen property. To actuate the annual income, multiply your figure by 12.

Deduct the expenses: Subsequently, deduct all expected expenses including any expenditure on property, taxes, renovations, and the mortgage on the property from your rental income. The cash flow of the property in question is the derived figure.

There are a lot of things you must be able to account for, all of which are essential in order to get the job done. Hence, despite the comparative simplicity of this formula, its effectiveness is totally dependent on your attentiveness because acknowledging the need for the subtraction of expenses is only a part of it; accurately calculating it is another huge and vital part of this equation.

Negative cash flow

A rental property is referred to as having a negative cash flow when in a situation in which the monthly rental spending on an investment property cannot be covered by the rental income per month. It is also called a negatively geared property. In other words, the inflow of money is worth less than the outflow of money for a duration of time. Hence, the investor loses instead of generating gains in real estate. In these situations, ask yourself how to revamp cash flow in order to prevent losses.

Positive cash flow

Positive cash flow is a situation whereby the property spawns a greater rental income than rental spending. Hence the inflow of money is worth more than the outflow of money for a duration of time. It is also known as a positively geared property.

For example, try to visualize owning a rental property that happens to be long term, and visualize it spawning a monthly income of about $1,200. After each month, all rental expenditure approaching $900 should be considered and provided for. Subsequently, the investor can then assuredly proclaim that his or her investment has gained a profit of $300 at the end of the month. It might interest you to know where you can locate positively geared properties, and these are explained below.

Typical Rental Property Cash Flow Sensors

A crucial step for estimating cash flow is in assessing probable expenditures. Disregarding any of the potential costs could alter the basis of the property's cash flow. Therefore, you must anticipate every cost and be mindful of them in order to meticulously analyze your expenditure.

Typically overlooked monthly rental expenditure is listed below.

Services: Prior to doing your summations, you should do a market survey to find out which service is regularly paid for. There are primary utilities included when purchasing a property and many landlords are very conscious of this. However, rentals are slightly dissimilar because you might be in a fix for quite a number of them. The tenant should be responsible for the calefactions, cables, and electricals. Nevertheless, property owners may choose to pay for the water and the septic tank. You may have to reach a compromise with your tenants in order to add other utilities for extra rent money.

Managing your property: Property management should be considered when estimating your cash flow even though most inexperienced real estate investors may manage their own properties in the beginning. Sooner rather than later, they will most likely begin to consider professional help because of lack of time, and the lack of the technical know-how to effectively manage the property. The fee is usually about 10% of the rent received per month. You can then make use of professional property management especially when your business starts booming and this is easier when you have planned for it.

Repairs: No matter how good a tenant is, it is inevitable to have needs for repairs such as a jam in the water closet, a busted dumping system, or gadget damage. It is advisable to reserve a small portion of your rental income just for the potential need for repairs.

Periodic expenditure: This area of expenses is probably the most ignored. Even though these expenses are only periodic, it's important to include them in your annual budget estimation. For example, if you have a property in an area that is easily affected by snow, it is important to have a snow removal system for winter. Consider including lawn maintenance, fireplace improvements, air units, and furnaces in your budget. Don't leave out costs for marketing when trying to get tenants. Marketing is a huge factor involved when trying to get tenants.

How do You Transform a Negatively Geared Property into a Positively Geared Property?

Some of the most successful investors in the real estate industry have given suggestions on how to succeed in real estate investment. Transforming your negatively geared property into a positively geared property is no walk in the park but it is achievable. Below are some tips to do this.

Cutting down the cost for sustenance: Never forget the golden rule, which states, "don't suppose your investment will be positively geared if you insist on lavishing money on furnishing and decor." You have to cut down on your costs, limiting it to maintenance if you are ever going to part from owning a negatively geared property to owning a positively geared property. We can understand why inexperienced investors would spend so much on decor and remodeling for an appealing outlook, but you must understand that the majority of tenants would rather do their own decor and furnishings, plus, they never expect anything lavish in the first place so start cutting down on unnecessary costs so you can start making actual profit.

Be your own manager: In order to do this effectively, you might require some schooling in the area of management and maintenance. You can be your own manager and avoid spending on professional managers. This can be a great boost towards becoming the owner of a positively geared property.

Modify your game plan: Your poorly planned strategy might be the reason you are still earning negative cash flow. According to the golden rule, don't expect your property to become positively geared if you are not planning on changing your game plan. You can verify that you as an investor have an excellent strategy by making use of a calculator called the Mashvisor's Investment Analysis calculator, or by conferring with successful and experienced investors in the real estate industry if you desire more knowledge on making the most powerful strategies.

Alternate lease terminations: Try to alternate the expiration dates of your tenants' leases so that you can always have abundant cash every month, as opposed to having abundant cash one month and being unable to make basic payments the following month. It is easy and tempting to want to make the expiration dates of the leases around the same time, particularly when your estate is in a university region and the schedule of events tends to reflect the timeline of the leases. Despite seemingly having more money, you should note that keeping your tenants' leases, and receiving the rent around the same time could cause a huge problem with cash flow. Try to alternate it to be sure you will never have too many vacancies, all at the same time.

Re-evaluate your deals: Investors in small-scale real estate tend to go about contracts the usual way. Stop to ask yourself how many times you have re-read your contract, and how long ago? Is the quality of the service you are getting worth the rate you are offering? How are your insurance premiums? Have they increased? Compare your interest rate with the already existing rates. When is the best time to recapitalize?

Check persisting expenses per month and figure out a way to obtain better rates for similar services. Even the littlest cut back on costs can boost overall cash flow.

A critical investment can be spawned from the earnings from cash flow on your houses. Your cash flow affords you the ability to settle mortgages and earn equity at the same time. Let us remind you that precisely summing up your income against your expenses from property investment is paramount to your advancement in this business.

Chapter 7

Preparing of Your Property For Tenants

It makes sense that a spotless and immaculate property will appeal to neat and immaculate tenants who will most likely keep the surroundings in the sterling state they met it. Put yourself in your tenant's shoes and try to recall all the things that mattered to you as you moved into a new apartment. So, while making the house ready, consider those things while also trying to avoid overdoing them. Be gentle on the decor, so you can give the tenant the chance to make their preferred choice. As trivial as it sounds, as time goes on, you develop a certain technique of knowing how to do enough while not doing too much in order to create a balance.

Enumerate everything you know that is essential, but you can only see these things by taking a walk around your compound. Some of these things could be:

- General appearance

- Interior decor

- Mending and renovations

- Improvement

- Security measures

- Items for defense

- Intermediary upkeep

Let your preparation start from the moment you drive onto your property. First impression matters, and in this case, it can be defined using two words, "curb appeal." It would be quite a shame and a waste of time if potential tenants can't even get past the appearance of the front of the house and lose any motivation to meet with you. Without doing too much, give the front a unique appeal in order to pull prospective tenants into the building. It's all part of the marketing strategy.

Carefully scrutinize any exposure to risks, and jeopardy to safety: In order to prevent any event of child mishap or misadventure, slips, and fire incidents, you should look out for the probability of these things as you survey your property.

Properly supervise the implementation of all gadgets: Do not forget about repairing faulty electronics such as ovens, heaters, and washing machines. Endeavor to assess every gadget in the house.

Eliminate stinks and mustiness: Be mindful of parts of the house prone to dampness and mustiness. These places include the washroom, kitchenette, wardrobes, and laundry. Don't forget to inspect beddings and rugs for mold and eliminate them by cleansing them with water and lather.

Clean the drapes, windows, and nets: Ascertain that these items are in satisfactory form, then get them washed, preferably done by yourself to economize. However, if any of these are broken, they should be repaired or restored as soon as possible.

Slather the walls with new paint: Sometimes, the walls will need to be repainted. You can paint the walls of your property on your own, as this will help you conserve funds. Nevertheless, don't fail to contact professionals if you are not sure what to do. They might charge a little over $400 for a room.

Substitute old locks and bolts with new ones: Endeavor to replace old locks around the house. I would recommend instating locks that could be programmed by the tenant with ease.

Recondition the air conditioning system: Ensure important parts, including the drains and plugs of the system, are in good condition by employing a maintenance person to revamp the system. If necessary, the entire system should be repaired and spoilt parts, replaced.

Confirm the renovation of floors made of woodwork: If you are really looking to lease out a property in an excellent state, then ensure you restore the floorings of the house. Shave off the finish if you have to or you could even repaint the wood.

Establishing an immaculate property will inadvertently set a standard for the tenant on how the house should be when returned.

Fumigate your property: The landlord is responsible for vermin control annually, especially if the tenant petitions for it. On the other hand, fumigating the house before renting it out automatically obliges the tenant to do the same before leaving. You might also need to flea spray if either you or the tenant has had pets on the property before or will in the future.

Spruce up the garden: Tidy up the garden, prune the yard, and shear the shrubbery to set a standard for the tenant, making them responsible for the upkeep and maintenance of the garden until they leave.

Chapter 8

Lease Agreements
for the Smart Investor

Lease contracts are legally binding, and they contain vital information and details of the agreement between the landlord and tenant, including the agreed monthly rent and the length of time the tenant is allowed to reside on the property. This contract is an agreement between the lease owner and the leaseholder to abide by a set of rules and regulations during their relationship.

Lease Versus Rental Agreement

These terms are usually mistaken for each other, but they mean different things entirely.

A lease is a long contract over a predetermined period of time, which can usually span between six months and five years, most commonly, for one year. The conditions and details of a lease are unalterable until expiration. There is no automatic renewal of a lease once it expires, therefore, you may both have to sign a new contract.

A rental agreement, on the other hand, is a brief contract. It is common for it to be over a 30-day period. If either party does not terminate the contract, then it will renew automatically at the term's end every month. The concerned party must render an officially written declaration at least 30 days prior (as requested by many states) to requested alteration, albeit either the tenant or landlord can alter the conditions of this agreement.

Whose signature should be on the lease?

Only parties above 18 years of age can sign a lease. It is extremely paramount at least two signatures to be on the lease: that of the lease owner or his/her agent, and that of the leaseholder. The number of signatures is dependent on the number of leaseholders above 18 years. Why are these signatures important?

If for example, a couple moves into your property but there are only yours and the husband's signature on the 1-year lease. This legally means that the only person accountable for the rent is the husband.

If soon after the husband departs for whatever reason, you end up losing because the wife is not legally bound by that contract, as her signature is not on it.

Who should create the lease?

Every real estate proprietor should have a lawyer who will cross check your lease form. There are quite a number of templates for free online. Your attorney can also spawn a new one for you as he is aware of state laws addressing housing and installments.

It is very crucial for your lease to be as legally precise and correct as possible for protection against confusion, mix-ups, or even a deliberate attempt at deception and manipulation by tenants who know how the system works and may try to poke at defects in your lease.

How long should the lease be?

The number of pages is subject to how much detail is provided. You should note that the more detailed your lease is, the safer you are from a legal attack, but never mistake a long lease for a good one.

Ensure that your lawyer is aware of every step you are about to take concerning your lease and use your previous experiences when spawning a lease. Rest assured that as you grow in the real estate industry, your experience inevitably grows too, thereby making your lease stronger, better, and more defensive against threats.

No matter how long the lease is or what style it is done, whether it is typed or not, it must cover some rudiments of the tenancy. Specific rudiments of a tenancy agreement should include the following:

- **The tenants' names and signatures**: The names of every adult moving into the building should sign. Couples, whether married or unmarried, should both sign the lease in order to make them all accountable for any legal breach in the contract in any event of a mix-up or misuse of property. In case of a misunderstanding between the tenants, you wouldn't be affected by the fall-out, as the agreement would bind whoever remains in the building to pay the rent. Also, it would be legally appropriate if you decided to cancel the agreement for all the tenants if any one of them breeches a term in the contract.

- **Occupancy restrictions**: This part of your agreement is important if you want the right to decide who and how many live on your property. Your lease should make it clear that the only approved people on your land are those whose signatures are on the lease, plus their underage children. With this part of the agreement settled, you can dislodge a tenant who moves in any other person not on the lease or rents out your apartment without your approval.

- **The term of a tenancy**: Your contract should indicate whether it is a rental agreement or a lease. As explained in the previous page, rental agreements are usually on a monthly basis and they are renewed automatically at the end of the month unless either party cancels the contract. However, leases most commonly run for a year. Ensure the document indicates the length of time you would like your tenant to occupy your property and your level of adjustability to the terms.

- **Rent**: Whether your contract is a lease or a rental agreement, it should contain the amount of rent to be paid at the beginning of each month. Also, indicate the means of payment (dispatch or at the office). Specify every detail to refrain from mix-ups. Details like:

  o Satisfactory means of payment (for example, transfer only).

  o If there is a penalty for a belated payment and how long the reprieve is before the tenant is expected to pay a penalty fee.

  o Penalty for bounced checks.

- **Deposits and fees**: Your contract should contain how much the deposit should be and when it should be returned in order to avoid the usual occurrence of altercations. It should include:

  o Amount of installment while abiding by state laws.

  o What the deposit is for and what it is not for. For example, it could be for repairs and damages or it can't be used in relation to previous rents.

o Calculate and make every necessary subtraction for when the tenant is about to leave. Specify when a deposit should be returned and how.

o Are there any non-refunds and for what reason? Be specific.

It may also be legally required of you to indicate where the security deposit will be held and if interest will be incurred and paid to the tenant.

- **Repairs and maintenance**: From the onset, in your contract, lay down every potential repair and who is responsible for what in order to prevent your tenant from withholding rent or from confusion involving the security deposit on account of damage he/she believes is your responsibility. Your agreement should include details like:

    o The tenant is responsible for the sanitation of the property and will be held liable for any damages caused by their misuse or carelessness.

    o Let there be a clear and detailed procedure that you will take in any event of a hazardous situation of which you are not liable if the tenant refuses to inform you about it.

    o Guidelines and limitations restricting the tenants from making certain amendments from the original design of the property. Clearly indicate these unapproved alterations in your contract.

- **Enter the rental property**: To protect yourself from trespassing charges or accusations of intrusion, clearly indicate the circumstances that will legally allow you to enter the building. For example, for renovation purposes. You should also assert how long the notice of entry should be provided before entry.

- **Limits to illegal activities by tenants**: You must include restrictions on any standard illegal activity by the tenants in your contract in order to evade being sued by the occupants of the buildings in the neighborhood and to evade altercations between your tenants. Examples of standard illegal activities include noise pollution, drug peddling, and human trafficking.

- **Pets**: Are pets prohibited? Indicate this in your agreement. If they are allowed, then put your restrictions on the number, breed, size, and littering. Indicate that it is the responsibility of the tenant to clean up after their pet(s) in the confines of your property.

- **Defacement and wreckage of the property**: Your contract should assert acceptable alterations and those that would require your consent. Ensure your agreement indicates who will be held responsible for any defacement to the building.

- **Other prohibitions**: Ensure your contract covers every possible legal prohibition that could put you in trouble in the future. Include details like the types of businesses that are prohibited from being conducted in the house. Parking rules and the use or misuse of shared areas in the property should not be left out of the agreement.

Hence, making sure your agreement complies with all pertinent laws and regulations, touching different sectors of violation including security codes, residence regulations, rent check rules, and anti-bigotry laws is vital. Take note of state laws previously mentioned in preceding chapters. Address rules for everything.

Chapter 9

Rental Property Sins
You Shouldn't Commit

It is a huge investment to purchase property with the aim of renting them out. Nevertheless, it goes beyond just getting people to take care of your mortgage.

It is very crucial for beginners and inexperienced lease owners to select their property wisely for the most profit. Being a newbie in the real estate industry can be detrimental to your growth if you do not have guidelines that will guide your decision-making and help you prevent making avoidable yet costly mistakes.

Below is a collection of some of the major things you must never do, assuming you will learn from them and not make these mistakes moving forward:

Underestimating the costs of repairs: Underestimating the costs of repairs can be a grave mistake. Don't be tempted by seemingly good deals, because they might just be covering up for the need for massive repairs before any rentals can begin. Falling for this gimmick can eat into your time and profits forcing you to increase your budget and lengthening the period you would have to wait for repairs to be completed before renting can be done. Inspect your prospective property to save yourself from stress.

Do you have questions on what to do when handling maintenance and fixings on your just bought property? Here are some tips:

- This has been stated before but I'll say it again: Be meticulous in your inspection of the property. Don't just walk through, be on the lookout for extreme damages, and never assume everything is okay.

- Don't try to save costs by hiring inept repairmen because you will end up spending more money than you should have in the first place. Instead, hire efficient and competent contractors for the repairs to ensure quality work will be done.

- You may not know a lot about the repairs that need to be done. Research and find out how it should be, and the standard costs before giving the job to anyone.

- Always add a little extra to your budget for overlooked problems in the house so you won't be caught off guard and unprepared when they suddenly appear. Some experienced investors have even advised on budgeting about 15% in addition to the initial budget for this kind of occurrence.

Be prepared, strategize way ahead of time, and be thorough when choosing. These can really help you in preventing future stress and unnecessary spending of your money.

Choosing a substandard neighborhood: The location of the property should be extremely important to you as it contributes to the appeal of the building to prospective tenants. Prioritizing the area your investment is located in is also part of your marketing strategy. It must be convenient to move to and from the house.

No matter how good the deal sounds, if it is in a bad and unappealing location, then it would pay off, in the long run, to turn it down. Never forget to research the neighborhood of a prospective property before purchasing it. Show more interest in the area, what is it surrounded by? Are there stores, restaurants, shopping malls, and nice houses? It's important you examine all these factors before choosing a property; trust me, it will pay off.

Look for property near trade or work centers because people will naturally tilt towards a house closer to their workplace. Finding a property in this type of location is what can then be referred to as a great investment.

Notwithstanding the seemingly good deals you come across, don't be in a hurry to choose, bide your time, research, and strategize for the best benefits and biggest profits.

Negative cash flow: It is natural to be elated about buying a new property, but if you are not aware or wary of potential mistakes, you may start losing before you start gaining.

Below are tips on how to prevent starting out with a negatively geared property:

- Stay away from areas with numerous vacant properties. This automatically devalues your property making it look like demand is poor. Invest in areas with huge demands, and seemingly low supply (fewer vacancies).

- If finding tenants is proving more difficult than anticipated, then feel free to adjust your rent for the time being instead of staying rigid and having no tenants for far too long. It is advisable to start "small" and earn less than you planned than to earn nothing at all. It gets better with time.

- Estimate the balance by deducting tax, mortgage, insurance, and renovations from the capital. If you do not have a reasonable amount remaining, then maybe that property is not such a great investment for you. Move on to another.

- Do not be bamboozled by how beautiful a house is. Don't let your sentiments cloud your judgment. Be sure to compare your prospective property with others to ascertain that you are not being cheated or paying more than usual for it. You will most likely not live on this property, so be very professional and handle the deal like the entrepreneur that you are. This is strictly business.

Overpriced costs for repairs and remodeling: Many beginners and inexperienced investors not only make the mistake of underestimating costs for maintenance, but they also tend to overpay for these renovations.

It is not advisable for a landlord to over-remodel. Granted, it is very important for a property to be attractive and inviting. It has also been established that making fundamental repairs and fixing basic things is essential, too, but do not make the mistake of overdoing it. That is not your responsibility.

It is understandable if new lease owners want their investment property transformed into a home of their dreams, but it would also be an unwise decision to try to make this happen. This would only make you spend much more money than you should, and waste time making renovations that may end up not even being your tenant's preference for decor. Be wise in your strategy, do enough renovations that will give just enough appeal to attract tenants.

Not doing your research: Many laws are required of property owners and if these laws are not dealt with skillfully, there could be serious issues in the future. Therefore, the need for efficient study and research before buying any property is vital. Listed below are things you must consider or pay attention to:

- **Rental license**: Get acquainted with the whole system of appealing for a rental license and how to get it.

- **Current specification**: Every state has different specified qualities for properties. So, ensure that your property has the current qualities as required by the state. There are higher uncertainties and cost in buying old properties, as this may prolong the time in which the property is made ready for occupants.

- **Safety**: The safety of your tenants should be assured. Note that carbon monoxide (CO) detectors should be placed in some areas of the property. The CO detector helps to detect the presence of carbon monoxide, thereby preventing CO poisoning. The property is properly examined, after which it is made accessible if the test is passed.

- **Habitability**: Your property should in all cases be "livable." Though there are different perspectives to this, you could refer to the state's laws regarding the habitability of your property.

If you really want to be a landowner, the above rules could save you a whole lot of trouble. Never forget to do your research and you will be fine.

Not covering all expenses: In a mortgaged property, the money paid as rent should absolutely take care of the debt. In addition to this, you will also cover the bills for maintenance, fixing or repairs, levies, and indemnity just as when you still inhabited the home. You might have to pay from your own personal earnings every month if the necessary bills are not covered.

Screening tenants: Accepting referrals is not such a bad idea, it could actually save you the stress of looking for tenants, but doing this without properly investigating the person's origin and history could be a bad idea. To do this, you don't need to be an undercover agent or cop, it can be done cheaply online but with the permission of the tenant. To get a hard copy of the investigation result, you must have written approval from the tenant. If after the findings you choose not to rent the property to him or her, write it in an official letter stating your reasons. When doing this, be very ethical and honest as the tenant has the right to file a lawsuit against you, if they feel that you are discriminating based on color, gender, tribe, or religion.

Make it official: Irrespective of whom you are renting the property to, a relative, a friend, even a roommate, it is very necessary to put everything in writing. Document the terms and condition, the rules and regulations required in order to save yourself from disputes with the tenant or roommate, mostly when your property is ruined or when the tenant refuses to pay the rent on time. In cases like these, ruined property or rent payment issues, the possible consequence should be clearly stated. The stipulated time for this outcome to be carried out should also be included. All these should be clearly written out and made official in order to avoid having issues with the tenant in the future.

Operating the security deposit: The operation of security deposit could differ for different state's regulations. However, do your research on what the government expects from you concerning security deposits. Getting money from the tenant without having an idea of what to do with it is very risky as you might be charged to court if the money is misused. Make findings to know if the deposit is to be placed in an escrow account for the tenant and if he/she is open to making profits.

Insurance problems: As a landlord, your home insurance might not cover your tenant. This can put you in a financial crisis if anything bad happens to your tenant or to your property while the tenant is still living in it. Therefore, it is necessary to put in order an efficient insurance policy that will cover harm done to your property by the tenant and cover you from legal responsibilities if your tenant should get into any unfortunate incident inside your property.

Too much responsibility: Being a landlord can be very stressful, time-consuming, and full of duty. Since a very reliable legal finesse is required to outline a standard rental agreement, tenants will always complain at odd hours, break rules at the slightest opportunity, be behind the date of rent payments, and other inconveniences. Handling all these alone is a huge responsibility. Too much responsibility? Yes, but they can be reduced by working with a skilled property management company. A good management group is familiar with all the fields of property management and will be able to take up your responsibility and you get to enjoy all the perks of being a landowner without any stress or worry.

Chapter 10

Maintaining Your Property

Having a property is one thing, but sustaining and keeping it relevant is another. Just like our skin, continuous nourishing, care, and regard is what keeps any real estate property glowing (successful). There are steps to sustaining your property, but the first step is having the knowledge on how to sustain it. Knowledge is power, so in order to be relevant in business, you must continuously upgrade your understanding of the real estate market. Remember a clean property that is well taken care of will always call for better clients and at a higher cost.

Some hints to sustaining your property are:

Be Ready

The cost of maintaining a property after it has been rented out is usually high. So you must be ready. The yearly maintenance cost is roughly 1.5 times the rental fee in one month. Nevertheless, this assessment differs for properties depending on the number of years and the living condition of the house. This amount takes care of the maintenance of the home all throughout the occupant's rent duration, until he packs out of the house. Also, while your property is not occupied yet, the house must still be in good condition. Therefore, make financial plans for sustaining the property, keeping it ready for a new occupant.

Routinely Inspect the Exterior and Interior of Your Rental Property

If your rental property is safe and free from any destruction, it will automatically enhance your profit and let you have hold of great tenants. Unexpected expenses like repairs and replacement can't be avoided when handling a rental property and you can't keep them unused. Below is a list of things to consider when supervising your rental property.

Exterior

- **Roof**: Run a check to know whether there are hidden shingles, destroyed flashing, or mold and moss. These put together can lead to expensive damages later in the future. Endeavor to note whether any tree limbs cross onto your roof and cut them away, as things like this around the home can be a discouragement to potential tenants.

- **Windows**: Carefully check to know whether all windows are closed properly with no spaces in between, and if any, seal them up. Tackling issues like this will prevent from heat loss and moisture destruction.

- **Exterior painting**: Ensure that the exterior of your rental property is painted often so as to guide it away from moisture and sun destruction. No one desires to dwell in a house that appears awful on the surface.

- **Landscape**: Look out for shattered tree branches or the ones containing fungus. That is, anything that could deter the safety and happiness of your tenants should be tackled and fixed. Moreover, ensure that the grass in the area looks green and frequently mowed so that any prospective tenants passing by could easily identify that your property is neat and properly looked after.

Interior

- **Water heater**: It's advisable to drain and frequently separate any dirt from the water heaters. If you reside in a location with a collection of small particles or sediment inside your water, then think of draining and consistently remove dirt as a monthly responsibility.

- **Smoke detectors**: This is an obligation. Examine that your smoke detectors have new and well-functioning batteries. Occupying a house without having an effective and properly functioning smoke detector can be very risky.

- **Heating and cooling**: Frequently check the heating and cooling system. Ensure that there are no plants growing within the filters, as it could stop airflow and may damage the system in the near future.

- **Paint**: Look around for mold or paint chippings that might appear as an eyesore on the walls and repaint for a fresh and clean interior.

Keep Your Tenants Happy

There are many ideas you adopt in order to maintain your property, but one of them remains that you should always try to keep your tenants fulfilled, rather than fixing damages every time. A check-up on them to know how they're doing or if they might need your assistance is enough. Such gesture will instill in their mind that you care and that their safety and satisfaction is your sole priority, which will surely make a positive difference. Your reputation with potential tenants will be strengthened and this will lure the right people into your rental properties. Answer their repair pleas. The reason most tenants pack out of a house is because they're not satisfied. Ensure you keep your tenants happy.

Hire a Property Manager

Protecting your rental property can turn out to be a difficult job. It's time-consuming and requires frequent attention. For people that see this as an overwhelming task, they can employ a property manager to take care of their real estate investment property. This is an effective decision though it's expensive; try to calculate the time it will save you. A real property manager can help you accomplish many things in real estate investment property, ranging from exterior to interior, along with handling monthly rent as well.

Follow the Landlord-Tenant Law

Adopting the landlord-tenant law will enable you to preserve your real estate investment property and support you in managing it effectively. This law will establish a foundation for you together with the tenant in order to avoid mistakes and protect your rental property. Maintenance is one of the obligations under the landlord-tenant law in which if followed accordingly, will help you achieve the desired result.

Renovate and Improve

Almost all tenants are often in search of new and advanced rentals. A property owner should frequently deliberate on ideas to help him/her renovate and boost real estate investment property. An example of this include putting together the latest style of exterior design, such as improving the yard or adding a garden, or, better yet, add current interior designs like frameless glass walls. Also, engage in research to find out trending interior designs that are less expensive. These latest advanced changes will surely lure tenants from across the globe.

Nevertheless, tenants also possess the right and freedom to enjoy a safe and comfortable living environment and homeowners are bestowed with the responsibility of protecting and preserving their property. A properly maintained property will lead to additional cash flow and success. Try as much as possible to sort out any rental property problems, before they get out of control.

Chapter 11

Marketing Your Rental Property

Irrespective of how nice the housing market is it can still take some time to get a tenant because you need to locate people with the perfect qualifications. Ensure that your marketing goes beyond the 'for rent' sign written on the side of the street. It would be good if you could produce a lot of eligible prospective tenants in order to enable you to rent out the property faster. Additionally, adopting online marketing together with the environment you work in will definitely present you with enough options and methods to rent your property.

The following are ideas to incorporate when marketing your property.

Step 1. Determine the appropriate rental price

Taking approaches like this is a vital step before you start marketing your property and endorsing a new tenant. You need to first do your assignment and carry out research on the rental market to understand the latest value before advertising.

It is necessary to set your rental price decision and whatever you conclude relies on your situation. You're supposed to identify the rental worth after buying the property. You may want to increase your tenants' rent to equal the market value. The following are methods to know your market rent:

- Purchase a local newspaper within the location of the available rental. Glance through the section with properties available for rent. Underline the ones that seem familiar to your own and make some calls so you can get to know the location and check it out yourself.

- Do some research on the Internet for possible rentals by indicating the city and type of rental.

- Reach out to a local property management company and officer to reward them for an hour or two of deliberation.

- Let the rental agent or property manager reach you at your property available for rent. The way to go about this is to agree to pay for the service.

- Visit a couple of local property management websites and find their possible rentals. They often issue addresses, and current rents combined with pictures of similar properties.

- Reach out to properties close to you from the 'for rent' signs positioned in the exterior of the units. Inquire from the person that responds to how much he/she is requesting for the rental.

Step 2. Clean and capture the condition

Carefully clean the area, snap plenty of pictures and record a complete video walkthrough. This idea will make listings unique. Make use of professional photos, because a simple search on Craigslist will show that most individuals don't apply the necessary effort in staging their pictures or snapping high-quality images. Some people don't bother getting rid of dirty laundry and other forms of stuff from the floor, which will deter the image. Bathroom pictures are combined with half-used toothpaste tubes mixed with missing caps, toothbrushes, open toilets, dirty towels, and broken bars of soap - things you never desired for your prospects to notice. To market your rental property, it involves painting a classic image for your potential tenants via your photos. This is because when your pictures are of a high standard, depicting every corner of the property clearly, the easier it becomes for prospects to check it out.

Again, if you detect anything that's not in accordance with the listings, endeavor to single it out. Opening up on some unfriendly items will surely develop trust.

For example, having a property built with interior heating and window space for air can be a no-go area for some people, but mentioning it will definitely save you from unnecessary displaying of such property. Wholesalers generally do important work in ensuring issues be disclosed, which on the other hand helps them establish an enviable trust.

Step 3. List everywhere

Develop a complete strike idea for listing your rental property. The following is a list of endowments that can be applied when developing an advertising strike idea. The most important goal is to develop a feeding frenzy of prospective rentals hunting for the property. The advantages peculiar to a feeding frenzy include:

- It helps you plan "open house" times without worrying about personal showings.

- It helps you qualify potential tenants better.

- Possibly, your property will be rented out faster by putting plenty of different ideas together.

The resources for a listing can be classified into one of six fun classes such as, Old, New, Short-Term Rentals, Organizational and Corporate, and Social Resources.

A. *Old Resources*

Most people don't consider old school methods to get tenants but it's very necessary to think about the demographic you're aiming for.

For instance, if you have one unit dwelling structures or houses in a fantastic area, with time, you'll also realize that an older demographic will desire to reside there.

Based on the studies from the Pew Research Center, the total number of persons who study local newspapers are above 55 years old. That's to say, the total number of people who will view your categorized advertisement will be above the age of 55. They could be more than willing to drive around searching for "FOR RENT" signs instead of browsing through the Internet.

- **Newspaper ads**: In all sincerity, this is not one I'd go for. Although, many people still read the newspaper to account for the investment, especially if you are trying to apply for a few vacancies.

- **Yard signs**: Whether you agree or not, this works well - mostly with one unit dwelling structures or single-family homes. Try to place another sign at the main junction showing them the direction to turn to. In addition, I suggest you purchase cheap signs in case they go missing.

- **Referrals from tenants**: Perhaps this only functions effectively if you have a cordial relationship with your tenants. A lot of investors use financial inducements such as $100 cash or gift card. This is a great idea if it minimizes vacancy time.

- **Referrals from friends**: This is a fantastic strategy. Most of your friends are aware that you have some properties for rent in a specific location. Anytime there's anyone searching for rental properties in that location, your friends could easily lead them to your rental properties.

- **Referrals from other landlords and investors**: This also is an effective tactic that can be adopted. You're probably a novice compared to most of your peers who are complete, or rather, full-time investors/landlords. Always assist them whenever someone is searching in a specific location where you're aware they own a property and they as well will render favor back to you when they can or when you ask.

B. *New Resources (the Internet)*

- **Postlets**: This allows you to keep your company details and data from other properties helping you save lots of time during the period you have new properties to rent out. The major upside is that it populates Trulia, Hotpads, and Zillow.

- **Craigslist**: An oldie but a goodie. Endeavor to fill every space provided including video walk and photos. You have no reason for avoiding such requirements and it actually helps in selling the property.

- **Zillow**: This is one of my recent choices. I don't get many leads as I do in Craigslist, but the leads here are of a higher standard.

- **Hotpads**: This is comparable to Zillow, but with a slightly clunkier Trulia. Due to some reason, I earn leads from people trying to resettle on this platform and it has fared well so far as a great resource for me.

- **Rent.com**: This is built and developed for big apartment owners, but it's made available everywhere and for all people, so it will soon be open for smaller players.

- **ApartmentGuide.com**: This is clearly designed and built for apartment owners. Most apartment managers maintain that it's a nice investment.

- **Realtor.com**: This site functions effectively when you're in emergency mode, to assist you in renting out your property. It might be expensive, but the work done is worth the cash.

- **PadMapper**: I don't prefer this site that much, only because many prospective tenants don't use it. However, I believe it has something great to offer in the future, thus, I still make use of it at times.

- **Facebook**: This involves part of the referrals coming from friends. Usually, I post a link via the Postlets listing, which makes it easier to be shared by friends.

- **YouTube**: In my area, I'm the only person that utilizes this idea, and people actually enjoy it. It helps me be in control of time while assessing tenants.

C. *Short-Term Rental Resources*

Most people have established a sustainable business emanating from short-term rentals, while a lot utilize it as the only hope. Personally, I have derived much fun with this kind of housing and I'm advising you to check it out.

- **Airbnb**: This is in all spheres my choice site. It's very simple to sign-up and equally easy to navigate both as a tenant and landlord.

- **VRBO**: This has been made available before Airbnb and gets more traffic as well. Nevertheless, it's harder to navigate. You would effectively utilize this site only if you were genuine about earning part-time money.

- **HomeAway**: People who have full-time vacation rentals really enjoy this site. Part of the HomeAway family of sites is VRBO.

D. *Organization and Corporate Resources*

Institutions that can afford the housing value of tenants such as nurses or lawyers are in existence. It is a reliable concept, one that is worth attempting.

- **Section 8**: Section 8 is the most common cause of controversy amongst other forms of rental properties. On one hand, you sort of get guaranteed rent. On the other hand, you will be in a terrible condition if the tenant is not qualified for section 8 and refuses to move out. The aim of this is that it's either all or nothing.

- **Churches**: Most churches are known to give transitory accommodation. If you own a fully furnished home, this is an excellent choice.

- **Non-Profits**: Special groups of people are supported by nonprofits and this can be an accessible supply of income.

- **Businesses**: Another method that can assist your stream of income is businesses that prefer paying rent ahead of time per annum.

- **Veterans Administration**: A superb organization. I've never worked with them but I'm ready to.

E. *Social Resources*

The simplest method of social media marketing for potential tenants is simply asking your followers and supporters if they know anybody who needs to rent a place or a house. Virtually, all investors I know use social media, notwithstanding, there are other numerous ways in which you can enhance this resource. There are different ways homeowners could exploit the social media resources, stated above, efficiently to their own advantage.

- **Facebook**: Videos are presently in high demand on Facebook. I'll encourage you to upload video rehearsals of your rental properties on your page. If you have multifamily properties, creating a Facebook group for your tenants will be a great idea. Also, try giving incentives for referrals in one major area.

- **Twitter**: The main aim of using Twitter is the search function. This function helps to find people that are looking for a place to rent in your area. Also, you can utilize the function of hashtags (#) to simplify the information in your feed.

- **YouTube**: Video walkthrough tours of my properties are something I've been practicing for a long time. This has reduced exhibiting it to people who do not like the features of some of my properties.

- **Google+ Hangouts**: You can also plan a live hangout with Google+ and create a walkthrough video tour and answer questions. Don't forget you can also do this with Periscope.

Step 4. Apply the tips below

To rent out your properties faster and to discover more qualified tenants, carry out these listed tips to quickly increase your marketing activities.

Choose your audience, choose your marketing: Ensure that your target is exact even if you do not have a specific target market. Know something about the area you're working in. What are the necessary things to take note of in the neighborhood? Who's moving in and out? It will not be difficult for you to find eligible tenants in need of a rental if your marketing objectives are targeted.

Use the right adjectives: To rent out your properties as fast as possible, be appealing and convincing to your audience through your pictures and words. While writing your advertisements, know that all the words used are of great importance. Using the correct adjectives to qualify your properties will bring about more calls from potential tenants.

For instance, if your property has double paned windows, energy saving appliances, or a programmable thermostat, you can simply describe your property as being green or energy efficient. These are simple words that potential tenants can acknowledge. Let your advertisements be exceptional and stay away from clichés. Don't write a book; rather paint an image for your potential tenants.

Get social: Social media now plays a powerful part in the presence of potential customers. Open social media accounts on all platforms especially those that specialize in visual content such as Instagram and Pinterest that can allow you to upload pictures of the properties and neighborhoods. Maintain a regular posting rate of numerous posts per week to sustain an effective online presence. Articles posted should be in tandem with the advertisements of your properties and related to industry news followed up with nice practices.

Use of word of mouth: Utilize people's point of views for your profit. Convince your buyers to write recommendations for your website and compensate them for referring friends to you. Offering adequate incentives will also help you obtain a positive vibe in the area, which will make it a lot simpler to get new tenants for your properties.

Develop your interest before searching for a market: Even if you are depending on renting out your current properties, try to plan ahead of time and draft out future plans. Create a mailing list that includes different communities to collate the list of passionate tenants. Create a relevant community content for the lists to allow your readers to understand every relevant area of the community. Make sure they know about properties that are on sale.

Network with the community: If your properties are located in one area, connect with the community deeply. Be involved in community activities such as assisting projects at the local school or getting a stall at the community festival. Tell people details about your properties during the community parade. When the people in the community know about your brand, you will be known as a great rental proprietor and locals will quickly refer you to friends and relatives moving into the area.

Market a community, rather than a property: People have different tastes so potential tenants will appreciate different resources, but everyone finds their community satisfying. This community is different from others due to tenants' statistics. A community consisting of good schools and daycare, affordable family activities, and serene neighborhoods will be for young families. Those meant for senior citizens could be defined by libraries, operative walking trails, recreation, and senior centers. When marketing a property, market the whole neighborhood and not the structure only, because the main thing the tenants regard is the neighborhood.

Advertise the right amenities: What you find appealing might not be appealing to prospective tenants. While taking an inventory of your property's assets or amenities, visibly review and think about what your prospective tenants will find appealing.

Energy efficiency as an amenity: If your property is green, having energy efficient appliances and windows informs your potential tenants in your advertisements that they will be saving money from cooling and heating expenses.

Social life as an amenity: The accessibility of your property to the rest of the city is an important amenity you should not forget. The hotspot points in the town and how far away or close they are to you, like shopping malls, five-star restaurants, etc. List how far away or close you are to these hotspots, including the public transit.

Chapter 12

Proven Ways to Capture
High-Quality Lifetime Tenants

Both good and bad tenants exist and sadly, there are no definite ways of differentiating the good ones from the bad ones. However, there are certain time-tested factors that can increase your chances of finding a good tenant for your rental. Listed below are seven helpful tips that can help you in making the best choice:

Have a checklist and set the right criteria

It is imperative to set your criteria before heading out in search of new tenants. For instance, how much income do you expect your potential tenant to earn monthly to be able to afford your rent price? What if your tenant owns a pet, will you still accept this tenant to live in your unit? If you have answers to these questions, it will make the tenant screening process easier and more effective.

Here is a sample copy of the recommended checklist for tenant criteria:

- ✓ Do they earn enough income to afford your rent?

- ✓ Do they own a pet?

- ✓ Do they have a stable job or is he/she a co-signer that earns enough income?

✓ Do they smoke?

✓ Do they have a history of paying their rent on time?

✓ Are they friendly and easy to relate with?

✓ Do they have a clean criminal record?

✓ Does their lifestyle fit your requirements?

Develop an online rental listing that sets expectations

When developing your online rental listing, you could add a paragraph describing your property. Doing so will allow your tenants to have an idea of what the screening process will involve for those who are interested in your property. Also, mention that a rental application will be required which will also require that they authorize a credit report as well as a background check.

Watch out for signs of danger at the property showing

There are certain things you need to watch out for during the rental property showing, i.e. the first time you meet a potential tenant in-person. Start by paying attention to whether tenants show up on time, if they meet your lifestyle requirements, and if they're friendly.

You could ask these additional questions to be sure if a tenant is a good choice for your property:

✓ What is your present living condition?

✓ Will you have roommates?

✓ Why do you want to move to another apartment?

✓ When do you wish to move in?

✓ How much do you earn monthly?

✓ Do you own a pet?

✓ Can I seek for references from your former employers and landlords?

✓ Will you tender a rental application?

✓ Will you agree to a credit and background confirmation?

✓ Do you smoke?

Potential danger signs to watch out for:

- The tenant shows up unprepared, is late, or fails to show up.

- Shabby appearance and their dressing are not well taken care of.

- They are rude or disrespectful.

- The potential tenant fails to complete a rental application or does not authorize a credit and background confirmation.

If the potential tenant answers all of the questions to your satisfaction and you don't notice any signs of danger, then it is time for you to move on to the rental application.

What to lookout for on a rental application?

A good rental application is expected to collect all necessary information about your potential tenant. I suggest you request for 5 years of residence history and the present landlord contact details. You could also request for employer history with contact information for employer references.

Here are 5 additional important questions:

- ✓ Have you ever declared bankruptcy?

- ✓ Have you been convicted of a felony in the past?

- ✓ Have you ever been evicted from an apartment?

- ✓ Have you ever failed to pay your rent?

- ✓ Do you smoke?

If a tenant answers **"yes"** to any of the above questions, then this could be a sign of danger.

Follow the law

There is a particular law that is designed to guide all landlords on how they must treat all prospective tenants equally. This is known as the Federal Fair Housing Act, which is to prevent discrimination against a certain group of people in any activity related to housing. In short, you cannot discriminate based on:

- ✓ Race or tribe

- ✓ Color

- ✓ National origin

- ✓ Religion

- ✓ Sex

- ✓ Familial status (families with children)

- ✓ Disability

Apart from the Federal Fair Housing Act, most states also have housing rules that apply to them, which you are expected to comply with, so ensure that you learn and stick to them.

Select a tenant who has good credit

Every landlord wants a financially responsible tenant. If a tenant is responsible enough to pay their personal bills on a regular basis, there is a better chance that they will also pay their rent when it is due. Getting a credit check involves cost implications, and most often, landlords ask their applicants to pay a fee for a credit check as well. There is a two-step procedure that is involved in checking a tenant's finances. They are:

- **Verify income**:

  o It's ideal to look for a tenant who earns thrice the monthly rent as income.

  o Request for duplicates of their pay stubs.

  o Call their employer to ascertain their employment status, employment duration, regularity at work, and monthly income.

- **Carry out a credit check**:

  o Do they have a good history of settling their bills when they're due?

  o What is their income to debt ratio?

  o Even if their income is thrice the monthly rent, you need to know exactly how much debt he/she has.

  o For instance: The rent is $2,000/month. A tenant is earning $6,000/month but has $3,500 in debt payments monthly. Despite their monthly income, this tenant may find it challenging to afford the apartment compared to another tenant making $5,000/month but owing no debt. The second tenant could be a good candidate to afford the rent despite their income not being thrice the monthly rent.

- o Dig into any past incidence of evictions, cases of bankruptcy, or civil judgments against the tenant.

Carry out a criminal background check

Criminal information is part of public record, and it can be verified at any of the various courthouses. This type of background check will reveal both minor and serious offenses committed in the past. What you need is the tenant's date of birth and legal name. Be cautious while doing this because those with a past criminal record might attempt to falsify this type of information, so be sure to get a recent and valid ID in order to verify that the information provided is accurate and true.

An intensive criminal check will include:

- A search into the Federal Court Record

- A search into the Statewide Criminal Record

- A search into the County Criminal Court Records

- A search into the Department of Corrections Offender Records

- A search into the Sexual Offenders Database

3 points of caution:

- Some states prohibit landlords from screening out tenants with certain criminal records. As a landlord, however, you may find a much easier reason to justify the rejection of a potential tenant. For instance, a tenant who abused drugs or one who had a violent criminal conviction can be rejected compared to a tenant with 10 speeding tickets. The reason is simply that a drug addict or a violent tenant can compromise the safety of other tenants.

- In addition, there is no publicly available national database of criminal convictions, thus it may be a challenge to conduct a thorough background check.

- Conducting a criminal check on your own can be a daunting task and is very time-consuming. It is often better to engage the services of a trusted tenant-screening firm to carry out the check for you. For an extra fee, you may combine this with checks on their credit records.

Dig into the tenant's rental history

Talk to about two to three of the tenant's past landlords if possible, because if they have a bad reputation as a tenant, the present landlord may want to send them off and may hide some facts from you.

Questions to ask:

- Do they pay their rent on time?

- Why do they want to move?

- Were they evicted for breaking rules or for non-payment of rent?

- Did they give a notice of 30 days before moving out?

- How did they keep their apartment? Clean or unkempt?

- Did they cause any damages to the apartment aside from the normal wear and tear?

- Were they respectful of their neighbors?

- Did the neighbors complain about them often?

However, if the prospective tenant is a recent graduate or a student, or a first-time tenant, they may not have any rental history. In this case, you may request for a co-signer before the lease.

Choose a stable tenant

Part of the information on the application form should include the tenant's past employment history as well as addresses. Do they move between jobs often? If they move often, will this pattern of movement be continuous such that you may have a vacancy on your hands soon? What if they do not have a stable job? This simply means that they may find it difficult to pay for the apartment after a few months, and you will have to start searching for new tenants and still deal with an eviction at the same time.

A maximum of two people per room

Although there's no laid down rules regarding the maximum number of occupants that are expected per bedroom, however, the more occupants you have per apartment, the more susceptible your investment is to wear and tear, and the more noise there will be. So as a rule, a maximum of two people is considered to be fair enough per bedroom as regards to the Fair Housing Act, but with the following exceptions:

- **State and local law**:

  o The landlord must follow any state or local housing codes if there are any.

- **Size and configuration of dwelling**:

  o A 500 square foot bedroom can accommodate more occupants than a 250 square foot room.

  o An apartment with a den and living room can house more people than an apartment without a den.

- **Age and number of children**:

  o If you refuse to rent out a bedroom to two adults and an infant, this could be seen as discriminatory, but if you refuse to rent a bedroom to two adults who have a teenager, this would be considered a reasonable excuse.

  o You may set a maximum limit of the number of people in an apartment, however you do not have the right to set the maximum number of children per apartment.

- **The setting of the sewer/septic system**:

  o If the system has the capacity to tolerate a specific number of occupants in the apartment.

Trust your instincts

It is very possible for you to do all the recommended screening procedures in the world, but at times, all you need to do is to trust your instinct as the best judge of character. Even if a tenant looks good on paper, you may feel that there is something off about the tenant. You may later discover that the tenant impersonated someone else while applying for the apartment. Although you should trust your screening, however, do not ignore your instinct.

Chapter 13

Keeping Tenants Long-Term

All landlords desire to have a tenant who is respectful, timely, and easy-to-deal-with. In truth, only a few landlords find such courteous and respectful tenants, and even then it can be difficult to keep them on the property long-term. Only a few landlords have come to the realization that their own actions could have a profound effect on the happiness and satisfaction of their tenants.

To ensure that you retain your tenant for a long time, ensure you make them happy and comfortable while in your property by making a few changes in the way that you manage the property or by improving your tenant-landlord relationship. Keep in mind that, a happy tenant makes the landlord happy!

Keep the property in good shape

To you, your property is an investment; however, the property is home to the tenant, and it is where they come to rest and where they spend time with their family. That is why it is imperative to keep the property in good shape. Carry out the necessary repairs and repaint it when necessary to do so. Also, ensure that you update/renovate the property thereby making it more desirable.

The fact that you don't live there doesn't mean you shouldn't pay attention to the needs of your tenants and their enjoyment of the property.

Describe the type of neighbors they will be living around, the social amenities in the community, and anything else you can think of. To attract the right tenant to you, they need to know as much as possible about the property. If you fail to mention some of these things beforehand, and they only found out after moving in, they might end up breaking the lease and you will have to start searching for new tenants.

Other important information that requires full disclosure includes cases of bed bugs, code violations, recent flooding incidents, etc.

Be warm and accommodating

If you eventually find a good tenant that pays the rent on time, who is well behaved, courteous and respectful of you, the neighbors and your property, then try as much as you can to not scare them off by being too hard on them. For example, if for any reason they failed to pay the rent on a particular month, be nice when they approach you to explain their reason(s).

However, you definitely will not want such excuses to become a habit, but if you notice they are a great tenant who is responsible and financially honest, then try not to ruin the relationship by punishing them for what was likely a complicated or unforeseen circumstance.

Perhaps at one point you also had bad days or sudden bills to clear, so try to be understanding when you can. There is a high possibility that your tenant will appreciate you more and will do the best they can to always make their payments on time.

Show some appreciation

The landlord-tenant relationship is a type of symbiotic relationship. While the landlord provides a tenant a place for the tenant to live, the tenant also fills the landlord's pocket with their money. And come to think of it, all landlord-tenant relationships are still business relationships, and just like in every business relationship, the landlord should show appreciation to their customers (the tenants).

For instance, during the holidays, you could give your tenant a gift basket or a card to show how much you value them. That way, they will see you more as a person and not just someone who only cares about cashing their checks. It also goes a long way to tell them that you're happy to have them around.

Another way to show your appreciation is to assist with seasonal costs, such as garden fees, or offering to pay part of their gas bill. This will make the tenant feel like the rental is their home and such a positive attitude is good for your business. In the future, when the property is up for rent, its good reputation will speak for it.

Be respectful to your tenants

All landlords are expected to give prior notice before entering an already rented property. It is often suggested to call your tenant before providing a notice to ask what day or time they will be available. After fixing an appointment that is convenient for you both, stop by to drop a formal notice.

It is rude for you to just drop a notice in front of their door for them to find the next time they are about to leave or enter the home. It is better for you to make your tenant feel like they are in control of who comes into their home, so instead of dropping a notice, next time try to communicate with them through the phone or by email so they too can have a say and feel in charge.

The fundamentals

Although all these might appear cumbersome, the goal is to retain the good tenants by keeping them happy and having them stay long-term. The key is to treat them how you would want to be treated. By doing this, they will not only be attached to the home that they have created, but also to the warm renting atmosphere that you, the landlord, have also created.

Ensure that your presence is a bonus in the rental relationship and not otherwise. Studies have shown that tenants who have good experiences while staying on a property are more likely to hold on to the property for a long time, and when it's time to move out, they will be glad to recommend you to friends and family.

Chapter 14

Managing Troublesome Tenants

Hundreds of dollars are spent to repair holes blown into the wall, damaged appliances, and bad odors that fill up the entire house. All these could be the price you pay for having a terrible tenant.

After the lease agreement has been signed and keys have been exchanged, we can only hope all will go well in your favor. Sadly, things don't always work out as we expect them to and dealing with an unpleasant tenant could be a real challenge. Below are some helpful tips that could help you in avoiding these types of tenants.

Bad Tenant #1: The Non-Payer

Have you ever had a bad tenant? That tenant who agrees to abide by the lease but fails to pay the monthly rent despite several ignored knocks on the door and missed phone calls. Such an attitude will make the landlord become more desperate and determined to acquire that check from the tenant at all costs.

If asked, a tenant could give the landlord endless explanations for why he or she is unable to pay the rent. Irrespective of the reason or excuses, the tenant is bound by law to make these payments. Unfortunately for the landlord, these missed payments can simply add up as sunk costs.

Possible Reasons a Tenant could give:

- ✓ Going through a rough patch in life, loss of a job, had a serious injury, a sickness that came with a high medical bill, or poor money management.

- ✓ Absent from an extended vacation.

- ✓ Planning to move out soon without informing you, forgetful, or simply irresponsible.

Managing the problem politely

Keep in touch with them: Try to reach out to them, their relatives, their office, or even their friends. You could also send a text message or email to find out what their situation is and why they are not paying their rent, or you could give them a call first to arrange a meeting.

But if you live close by, you could approach them for a face-to-face conversation, but it would also be fine to give them a message (at least 24 hours) to notify them that you'll be visiting. Once in a while, go onto the premises and check, try as much as possible not to be rude. That way, you'll be able to know if they've been gone for a long time or if they are planning to move out.

Talk it out: If you notice that a tenant has not been able to catch up with their rental payments for some months, it is recommended that you have a face-to-face discussion with them. Let the tenant know the legal implications and the consequences of their actions if they fail to clear all their rental payments, which could include forced eviction. Once they realize the gravity of their actions, they will be more likely to take positive steps to make their rent payments.

Discuss their financial status:

✓ How much is your monthly income presently?

✓ Are you sure you're financially capable to pay the rent?

The terms of eviction depend on the conditions of the agreement as stated on the lease. For instance, the terms of the agreement could permit you to evict the tenant for failing to pay last month's rent and could also give you the right to retain the security deposit as a compensation for your loss.

Bad Tenant #2: The Late Payer

Another set of tenants are the tardy payers who are a bit better than the non-paying tenants, the only problem is that they may not pay their rent on time. Like the non-payer, they may also ignore the landlord's calls and messages. However, unlike the non-payer, they pay their rent at the end of the day, which is the most important thing. But such delayed payments could give the landlord a wrong impression of the tenant.

The lease agreement should include the monthly deadline as well as the grace period during which a tenant is expected to make rental payments. Once signed, the tenant is legally bound by law to abide by these rules of the legal contract. For instance, your lease agreement might have stated that an additional fee will be charged for late payments. However, the tenant may not even bother to pay both the rent and the late fees.

The delay in payment will make it hard for the landlord to plan his or her budgets and then tags the tenant as unreliable. Although the tenant will still pay their rent despite the delays, the landlord still has a valid reason to obtain a late rent notice or even eviction notice form.

The tenant's excuses:

- Forgetfulness and irresponsible attitude.

- An unforeseen occurrence, causing delayed payment.

- They're having a hard time getting the money via loans.

Managing the problem politely

Talk it out: Start by sending a message or email where you will emphasize why it is important for the tenant to abide by the agreement stated in the lease, and if they fail to comply, they will have to face the consequences such as forced eviction. Try as much as possible to be sure to meet with them face to face in order to ensure proper communication between both parties and that the message is clearly passed on. You could also ask the following questions:

- What event is responsible for the delay in payment?

- Are you aware that as stated in the lease agreement, your rental repayment is due on a particular date of each month?

- Are you financially capable to pay the rent payments when they're due?

Once you've clarified these points, go over the lease agreement again with your tenant. To determine what to do next, try to examine the present circumstances and if the incidence is a one-time occurrence or a bad habit. It's up to you to use your discretion whether to give your tenant one more chance to pay on time or to extend the grace period.

Bad Tenant #3: The Rule-Breakers

As a tenant, there will always be guidelines that you're expected to follow, whether those stated in the lease agreement or an additional set of rules which the property manager deems fit to add. Most landlords make the mistake of assuming that once the documents have been signed, tenants have to think twice before breaking the rules. However, there are some tenants that don't give a damn; they just break the rules at will.

For instance, the landlord may place a strict "no party" policy, but who will stop the tenant from inviting friends over for a TGIF night? In most cases, the landlord may not discover that the tenant is going against the terms and conditions of the property until probably after some weeks or months when the trashcan is filled with empty cans and bottles of beer. Another example can be that the landlord is against subletting; still, the tenant went ahead and sublet the unit to someone else, a stranger. Such an action could warrant serious legal actions against the landlord and the tenant alike, which is one situation that every landlord wants to avoid.

The tenant's excuses

- He/she didn't have time to carefully review the lease agreement.

- Negligent, carelessness, and irresponsible.

- Surrounding circumstances, they had no choice (e.g. perhaps a friend or family member needed a place to stay).

Managing the problem politely

At times, it is often difficult for you as a landlord to determine if the rules have been broken or not unless you pay a regular visit to the property to see how things are going. But even after discovering that they're breaking your rules, you will still need to handle the situation carefully.

Have a face-face meeting with the tenant. Presenting these matters to your tenant is the key step to finding a solution.

You could discuss the following:

- Does any tenant have another way out for what he is doing?

- Will it be necessary to add an extra addendum to the lease, such as a partying addendum or a subletting addendum?

- If there are any damages done to the property, the tenant must be held responsible and should pay for it.

- Go over the lease agreement once again and enforce the rules and regulations as well as the consequences. Also, make all necessary clarifications.

However, if the tenant lives with other roommates, why not talk to them and see if they could also assist with enforcing the residential rules. Alternatively, you can even recommend a roommate-to-roommate agreement to see if that too could aid the process.

Bad Tenant #4: The Destroyer

This group of tenants causes damage to the property either intentionally or accidentally. Many landlords have complained bitterly about tenants that make it a habit to damage property intentionally. These types of damages not only cost the landlord hundreds of dollars but also bring sadness to the heart of the landlord.

The tenant's excuses

✓ Mental illness.

✓ Carelessness, immaturity, or irresponsible behavior, which led to an accident.

Managing the problem politely

Start by estimating the cost of the damages they caused, then decide whether the tenant will be responsible for all the costs. Arrange a meeting with the tenant and iron out the following issues:

- Will the tenant be able to pay for and repair the damages?

- How can similar incidences be prevented from happening in the future? What was responsible for the damages? Did the tenant intentionally set the house ablaze again? Do they always forget to turn off the stove? Did the garden get burned after a barbeque party?

- Would there be any need for the tenant to buy a tenant's insurance?

Of course, you cannot send a tenant packing without a legally valid reason, but the lease agreement is more than sufficient. As long as the tenant has broken the rules in a legally binding document, the landlord has valid reasons to send him out of his or her property.

What can you do as the landlord?

✓ Before accepting new tenants, first conduct a thorough background check on the prospective tenant. Using software applications that can help screen prospective tenants in order to fish out the bad ones can do this.

✓ Also, see to it that the tenant signs the lease agreement in order for you to be able to enforce the written rules and expectations.

✓ Set up a face-to-face meeting with the tenant to enforce the rules and regulations as well as what is expected of both parties.

✓ Be sure to have an escape plan in case the tenant is not living up to your expectations. For instance, you could evict a troublesome tenant if they float the lease or you could possibly wait till the agreement expires then you terminate it if necessary, without renewal.

Landlords are not perfect, and they may not know what kind of tenants they are dealing with until after they've leased out their property. But, try as much as you can to clearly spell out the expectations of the tenancy and itemize the consequences associated with breaking the rules in the lease agreement. As a legally binding document, the lease can protect both parties from an ugly situation.

Six Smart Ways to Get Rid of a Bad Tenant

Getting rid of troublesome tenants can cost thousands of dollars in terms of unpaid rents, repairs for damages done to your property, cost of court eviction, and payment fees for an attorney including the amount of time that will be wasted.

The best thing to do is to avoid such ugly situations entirely, preventing it as much as you can. Sadly, most landlords assume that prevention starts and ends with tenant screenings. Rather, as a landlord, you need to send a persistent message each month that will make them know that you take the lease terms seriously and you are ready to enforce them without delays if they fail to meet up.

This requires that you conduct regular inspections, tender lease violation notices ASAP, and check in with them regularly to discuss maintenance, and most importantly, serve them an eviction warning notice from the very first day the rent officially expires.

If you can adhere to all the suggestions stated above, I can assure you that you will prevent 99% of tenant-related headaches. Still, how about the remaining 1% of cases, those stubborn tenants that just don't play by the rules?

Before the do's, let's take a moment to outline the don'ts.

The Big No-No: Self-Help Evictions

Let it be known that a self-help eviction is completely illegal. It's not just a slap-on-the-wrist penalty, but also a real-time jail term.

Self-help eviction is any action taken by the landlord in order to make the property unsuitable for living, thereby coercing the tenants to vacate.

Such actions include, but are not limited to:

- ✓ Changing all the door locks.
- ✓ Cutting off utilities.
- ✓ Blocking off physical access to the property.
- ✓ Breaking in and removing the tenant's belongings.

✓ All forms of harassment.

By law, there is only one legally justified way to forcibly evict a tenant from your property and that is by filing for eviction in the court of law.

Apart from filing an eviction, what are some alternatives?

Below are 7 creative ways of getting rid of an unpleasant tenant. They are outlined in increasing order of urgency.

Increase rent: Do you have tenants that adhere strictly to your lease agreement, yet are very annoying?

For instance, they may cause a nuisance to the neighboring tenants or call you every time to ask you to fix minor repairs such as changing a light bulb.

In such situations, you will notice that your tenants haven't violated your lease, but you just want to get rid of them. You can try raising the rent "significantly" when it's time for a lease renewal.

However, ensure to conform to your local and state laws before increasing the rent because the percentage of increment in some jurisdictions are regulated by law, and therefore the law restricts landlords from suddenly raising the rents in a single hike.

Another caveat states that you can't increase the rent before the expiration of a fixed-term lease.

Keep in mind, however, that this method is not always guaranteed to get rid of your tenant(s). What if the tenant(s) agrees to pay the higher rent?

At the end of the day, it's still a win-win for you because the extra cash will compensate for all your troubles.

Do not approve their lease renewal: You are not obligated to approve the renewal of your tenant's lease... or are you?

Take caution: Some laws that are in favor of the tenants make landlords accountable for the non-renewal of their tenants' lease.

Most times, you can just send a civil, formally addressed notice stating the reasons for the non-renewal of the lease. Appreciate them for the period they spent as your tenant, clearly state your policies for vacation (and an assessment of the condition of vacation), and make sure to point out the ways that they can make sure that there is a refund of their security deposit.

Most importantly, ensure to deliver notices for non-renewal within the legally stipulated period in your state. It might be 1, 2, or 3 months.

Confirm from the jurisdiction governing rentals or landlords in your state (or get a lawyer to do this).

Assist them in locating a new home: Although it might come across as unreasonable, if you want your terrible tenant to leave quickly, you may have to assist them in locating a new place of residence.

Present offline brochures or websites to them to locate and assess listings. Highlight local community services that assist individuals in finding a place of residence. Assuming their terrible attitude is not innate, and your property was just not the right one for them, you can make inquiries from local clubs or groups, or even other landlords, concerning information on the units that might be available in future.

You must be careful not to ruin your relationship with other landlords and shareholders. Do not make up a false history for an applicant. Rather, simply make a positive recommendation, as long as the landlords are not deceived.

Make it clear that you do not mind taking legal action: The fact that you cannot send a thug to scare them does not stop you from threatening them (all right, that is a bit too much, but you understand what I mean). You simply must ensure that your "threats" are within the legal restrictions.

Employ the services of a lawyer, or over a few drinks, convince your friend that *is* a lawyer to send a letter that is intimidating enough to your tenants. Scare them with lawsuits, collections, and ruined credits.

Write an honestly brutal letter to them: There is a huge price to pay if they refuse to leave in peace or if they do not fix the violations of their lease.

This strategy is very effective only when you have previously made it clear that you do not tolerate violations in the lease agreement by serving a notice for eviction the moment the rent is delayed.

You must submit one in court immediately after the compulsory waiting period is over.

Consider serving this menacing letter the very day you file for an eviction in court.

"Today, I filed an eviction notice in court. I hope we can fix this without subsequent legal action; however, you are to expect these legal actions if there is no resolution of your lease violation."

Then provide the evidence for these threats!

Propose a cash payment for keys: This might prove difficult, but it is efficient (it might even be the most efficient) way of kicking out terrible tenants from your assets.

Supposing a complete eviction is about $4,000 and might take at least 3 months, it is cheaper to provide an incentive of $500 to your tenants so that they can relocate by the coming weekend, isn't it?

This means that you are encouraging their terrible attitude by paying. But the thing is, do you recall the legal actions discussed previously in that threatening letter? Most times, it is cheaper to let go of the losses than to pursue irresponsible tenants.

The legal system encourages the bad attitude of tenants. These laws are tenant-friendly, and not at all in favor of the landlords. If there is a delay in the payment of a tenant's rent, for a few months they are allowed to remain without paying rent while you are delayed for various reasons in the eviction court. Or, they can accept your proposal and vacate without any delay.

Whatever happens is in their favor.

For a lot of landlords, this might be very difficult to come to terms with. Therefore, it is necessary to avoid this if possible.

One extremely important precaution when proposing payment for the keys is that you must put down stringent rules. They would only be paid if the property is left without any dirt or damage whatsoever; in the same manner that they are required to leave it assuming they were going to receive a refund of their security deposit.

However, the laws are not in favor of the landlords. Again, the laws are tenant-friendly.

This is the major reason you are settling for this approach: If you serve a regular eviction notice, I can almost assure you that they would leave your property in a despicable state.

Search for (and include evidence) for illicit dealings: Are you prepared for the most brutal approach to evict bad tenants?

A point consistently reiterated in this book is the persistent execution of the lease agreements. I've mentioned routine assessments of your rental unit. This is another reason to do them: A lot of states and districts support facilitated evictions if your tenants are not compliant with the laws.

Agreed, you are still required to send a previous notice before entering your rental property. So, your tenant might stay at home when you arrive, making it harder to search for and provide evidence for any illegal dealings.

However, landlords can also enter their properties based on maintenance and repairs, and not only for assessment of their properties.

Consider having your visiting hours during your tenant's working hours.

However, you must be careful so that you do not go beyond the limit. You are not allowed to rummage through your tenant's unit. Simply opening and closing their closets can be regarded as a violation of their privacy. But it is amazing how inefficient a lot of people are at hiding their drugs and baggage.

Take pictures (with the timestamp activated), and bring it to the notice of the local cops and serve the appropriate eviction for illicit dealings.

A Word of Caution

Your plan should always include a regular, legal eviction. With the use of court filings and earning eviction notices, send a clear and definite message to your tenants that you do not tolerate violations of your lease agreements and there are serious consequences if they are violated.

After all that has been discussed, evictions take a lot of time and money. Yet, it still comes with a lot of allowances that enable "professional tenants" to increase their stay on your rental property.

The strategies that are highlighted are concordant. Depending on the case, you can use these strategies and file a normal eviction.

However, do not expect that your tenant would leave without any fuss. Properly document every record and gather your paperwork, while expecting your tenants to strike in court.

Most importantly, you can prevent this from happening initially by a rigorous screening of your tenant and constant enforcement of the lease. An iota of prevention will ensure the regular payment of your rents and the conservation of your properties from damages.

Chapter 15

Increasing your Portfolio of Properties

Being a rental property investor can yield profits in the long run. Though making profits while renting properties can be quite stressful. The acquisition of one or two properties is pretty simple, but if you are looking to make a fortune from investing in properties, it is really not enough. You must put in a lot of time and be consistent in developing your rental assets. You need the proper business development techniques to successfully purchase many rental properties.

Below are 8 suggestions for expanding your rental property business.

Get Additional Education on Real Estate

Quality real estate education is one of the major requirements for the expansion of your rental property business. Although you do not need a degree, you still need to acquire the necessary skills and education.

Concentrating on getting additional real estate knowledge would make it more likely for you to succeed.

You might be coming up with an investment strategy for your property, choosing the real estate approach that is most suitable for your investment, picking out the financing of your investment property, or screening future tenants. Therefore, you need the proper knowledge.

Being the owner of a rental property might have made you more knowledgeable concerning some things; however, the ownership and management of many properties is a different ballgame.

It would be difficult to own more than a few rental properties if you do not increase your knowledge of real estate. Once your "education" has ended, it is unlikely that you would succeed in real estate investment.

Get more knowledge on real estate by registering for classes online, studying important books, real estate journals, news on real estate, and so on. Getting a real estate mentor to help is also a good idea.

Consider a Real Estate Partnership

It is very expensive to buy many rental properties. Substantial capital is required for making the down payments and additional property costs that might have been incurred in the process. These costs might be too much for most people. However, you can still expand your assets by supplementing it with leverage.

If you are skeptical about getting loans from moneylenders or banks, you must look for a business partner to make the capital available. Instead of waiting for some years just to save enough money, your business can develop at a faster rate with a dependable partner that provides the capital. You and your partner can put your financial assets together to purchase rental properties.

Aside from financing your real estate investments, a partnership also enables you to share your responsibilities. This ensures the growth of your business, as well as the proper management of every part of your rental property investments.

Become an Expert in Investment Property and Market Analysis

One other relevant suggestion to expand your rental property business is the acquisition of the skills required to carry out the analysis of both the investment property and the real estate market when purchasing a rental property.

You might be making a lot of profit presently, but you need more for the expansion of your business. The success of your rental property business would be determined by the factors affecting the economy, like jobs and median income.

You need to do a thorough analysis to discover information regarding your rental properties and target market because once too many units are unoccupied, your profits start to diminish.

Too many properties with negative cash flow are bad for your business.

A few investors in real estate have a preference for markets that are close to their homes. Do not be misled, however, into thinking that the only profitable rental market available is your local housing market. In some cases, purchasing a property in a different state might pay off. An analysis of the real estate market would efficiently help you recognize this. You would be able to recognize the target market that would yield more profits. As soon as you have identified the right target market, get down to neighborhoods.

The next stage is to upgrade the rental property for subsequent assessments. Investors in real estate are required to carry out a thorough analysis of investment properties to save costs and generate positive cash flow.

Hire a Real Estate Agent

Although a few real estate investors might decide to do it on their own, employing a real estate agent might be useful.

Employing a real estate agent that is experienced in the purchase of investment properties can guide you towards making the right choices. A real estate agent can also provide suggestions on how to expand your property rental business.

However, it can be very difficult when you try to manage your real estate business alone. If there are a lot of deals to be examined, a real estate agent can help you to analyze these.

Although it is pertinent to employ real estate agents that are experienced in a specific market, the implication of this is that you may require the services of more than one real estate agent.

Get a Property Management Professional

A few investors in real estate might prefer to personally handle their real estate properties. Though this is not always effective, particularly if you are very busy.

Once your real estate assets start to expand, you might have to employ qualified professional property management. Your investment properties, involving repairs, maintenance, tenant screening, and other important dealings would be taken care of by a property manager. This would help to create more time for you, and you would be able to use that time to acquire additional properties.

Diversify Your Investments

Another relevant suggestion on how to develop your rental property business is diversification. Like any business, it is not financially safe to have only one kind of business. There are fluctuations in the real estate market. You would be gravely affected if the market drops, and all your investments were in that market or real estate business.

But, investing in other things can minimize your loss. Other investments that are yielding profits can make up for investments that are not generating cash flow.

When your rental properties in other markets are yielding profits, that money can be used to purchase additional properties.

This makes the expansion of your real estate investment quicker. Thus, try to invest in various locations and utilize various techniques.

Let Your Investments be Focused

Discover the most suitable method to make profits from a property and become very skilled at that method.

You can choose to purchase dilapidated properties and renovate them, or to increase the interest, and then put them up for lease. After you raise the rental profit and generate positive cash flow, you'll have enough interest to borrow from to facilitate further investments. You can choose to purchase blocks on a piece of land and build them yourself.

Regardless of your investment approach, being focused helps you to make additional profits, and instead of trying out everything, you will become skilled at one particular thing.

Look for a suitable investment approach, and then try to do a comprehensive study. Attend seminars, read relevant books and get involved by investing and trying out your method. Continue learning and improving.

Interest-Only Loans

I would not recommend that you use non-amortizing loans since I am not a financial expert; however, I can give you a very apparent (but still underestimated) advantage of using non-amortizing loans that might enable a few investors to acquire additional property.

Non-amortizing loans minimize your expenses, thus, generating positive cash flow. Raising the rent fee is not the only method of generating positive cash flow; minimizing your expenses also helps you generate positive cash flow.

Consider the amount you would save on a loan of $300,000. Loaning $300,000 at 8% per annum interest-only loan will require the interest of $461 per week and a principal and interest loan (for 25 years) will be at a cost of $534 each week. You get to save $73 each week and $3,796 each year.

If your income for each year is $45,000, your income after the tax deduction is increased by 10%. The $3,796 can be used to obtain a new loan or deposited in other savings. Also, it might differentiate between negative cash flow and positive cash flow.

Ensure that you discuss interest-only loans with a professional accountant or a financial expert, however, think of them as a method of minimizing your expenses.

Eventually, once the rent starts getting higher, you can upgrade to principal and interest loans, from interest-only loans. This makes it possible for your tenants to redeem your loans without you even having to spend a dime.

You can purchase more than one or two properties. You just need to be clever, make a wise investment, and persevere. Think about the financial profits that would be gained from getting rents from about 10-20 properties. This can be accomplished if you act on these suggestions.

A lifelong view on investment - Do not ignore what you are being told by the market.

In the world today, we are programmed to search for the immediate fulfillment of our desires. Whatever it might be our wish must be fulfilled immediately. This is definitely what happens regarding real estate investments. If you look for a real estate show on TV, you are sure to find several programs involving home flipping.

It is totally understandable if you are trying to make quick profits, but there is a different method of real estate investment. A few real estate investors buy and hold properties to expand their properties. This might not provide the immediate satisfaction that you would otherwise get from flipping, but in the next five to ten years, these could pay off. The market presently favors the renting of properties for long-term.

Several years ago, if you were to purchase a house, you would be the owner for several years. A lot of people who owned homes regarded their properties as a method of compulsory savings. They might reside in the house for thirty years, and following the settlement of the mortgage, they can live in comfort after their retirement.

The way we regard our properties has been altered by the quick appreciation of these properties, but the principles guiding the ownership of a house are still unchanged. If you make a purchase now, while putting the future into consideration, you would eventually make more profit.

Rather than making fast profits through home flipping, selling in the future can provide you with five times more profit.

Equity development and cash flow are the two reasons why an investor might own a rental property. As determined by the down payment, rent, and the property itself, it is possible to profit in both ways. If you own a property that has minimal expenses and generates high rent, you should see the advantages of cash flow each month.

This profit can be channeled into the purchase of additional properties, paying off debts, or to any aspect of your business.

The higher the cash flow, the higher the value of the rental property. Although you might not get thousands of dollars in cash flow, you can expect a few hundred. If you spend this money reasonably, your investment business will expand rapidly.

A few investors regard rental properties exclusively as long-term assets. In this case, the cash flow each month might be insignificant, but this does not matter to them. They do not mind getting a small amount of cash flow each month for a valuable property that would yield even more profits in the future. They are sure that the property would still be in their holding for 5-10 years and they are not bothered by the cash flow each month, or how valuable the property is, presently.

Their tenants are used to pay their mortgages and raise their equity. They have made purchases in areas that are potentially valuable, and rather than selling for little profit, they do not mind waiting 10 years to fully start reaping the benefits.

Although in the last five years, the market has become more stable, but profits have still not skyrocketed like they were predicted to. There are fluctuations in the rental market. Eventually, there would be a consistent increase in demand, followed by a rise in the values of the rentals. By patiently waiting for that time, experienced investors in rental properties can have maximum profits from a property rather than making temporary, fast profits.

Paying down the accrued equity on a property makes many options available to you. The main goal is to attain complete ownership of a property and receive complete cash flow; however, not every investor is patient enough. A zero balance is not required for you to pull cash out of your property. If your payoff were made quicker by making additional payments every year or holding the mortgage for 10 years, there would be a significant reduction in your debts. Along the way, there might be an increase in the value of properties, and you would have the chance to take out some cash by refinancing, or request for a second mortgage on your property. If there is a reduction in the balances of your mortgage, your monthly payment will still be low, and you will be able to take out the cash required for other projects and receive cash flow each month. Having a lower balance increases the options made available to you.

The most profitable real estate assets are a combination of short-term and long-term rehabilitation. Throughout the nation, it has become very difficult to save enough for retirement. It doesn't matter if you still get some profit, you might not have enough for retirement. A solid portfolio of rental properties can make your retirement very comfortable, and it might even happen earlier. Although you might think 10 or 20 years is too far away, it is approaching faster than you can imagine.

There are a few investors that put up valuable rental properties for sale before their peak values, just to obtain a temporary profit. If they had endured the hard times that are experienced by all landlords and withstood the temptation to sell for a quick profit, they could have become owners of properties that would be beneficial after retirement. It can be quite difficult to hold a property long-term, but if you try, it will pay off eventually.

Chapter 16

Tips for Survival in Real Estate Investment

Assuming you have not tossed this book over the bridge closest to you or charged out from a room screaming, the business of real estate is possibly suited for you!

Simply keep in mind that the secret of success in any form of dealing is to reasonably take risks. This implies that you must attain a degree of understanding to recognize opportunities and risks for eventual success.

Make a down payment of your loans with the highest rate

A few investors make efforts to pay down mortgages than the limited stipulations in the notes. If this is what you have decided to do, try to pay down the notes with the highest rates of interest, in order to save money. If there is an economic decline, you might consider refinancing the term, to reduce your payment each month. You can increase the capital to be paid later and reduce the note terms when the market becomes more stable.

Purchase Reasonably

The analysis of a building comprises of the integrity of the structure, current and deferred requirements for maintenance, performance, characteristics, advantages, and the appearance.

The financial performance comprises of the rental history that includes the turnover rate, vacancy rate, and cap rate, then, the investment returns.

The economic analysis comprises of social factors, political factors, the local economy, the demographics, and rate of crime.

You must carry out the relevant studies to guide you on your investment plans.

Make inquiries, speak to other investors, and take a drive around the surrounding areas to get a feel for the neighborhood. Quality studies require a lot of time. If you know that the neighborhood is presently not the greatest, consider holding the investment while hoping that there will be a change.

Take note that taking a risk is fine; just be sure of what you are involving yourself in. Make proper negotiations and be prepared for any unfortunate event.

Avoid Over Leveraging

Investments with complete leverage do not make allowance for maintenance projects, unoccupied rentals, economic decline, or other hidden costs. Paying down is beneficial.

Over time, lenders have acquired the knowledge and experience that is required to avoid failure in their investments. The banking industry requests for mortgage insurance that are more than 80% LTV (loan-to-value). They know the increased risk that might result from properties with a low down payment (or high leverage). In most cases, the success of the bank is guaranteed with a loan that has 80% or less loan-to-value. There is a 25% down payment requirement in multiple family properties or properties that are not occupied by the owner so start making preparations.

After choosing and analyzing the vacant properties, and you have recognized the best 2 to 3 choices, take some time to consider the fate of your investments if there is a 25% reduction in the price of rent, or if the local employer decides to relocate or close up their business.

Look out for the indications of a recession

The earliest indications of an impending recession are overbuilding, a tenant's relocation in order to minimize costs, low inquiries from people relocating from a different location or state, fluctuations in the stock market, fall in interest rates, downsizing of companies, etc. You can closely monitor changes in the economy by reading your local newspapers for an increase in the number of advertisements for identical rentals, price variations in identical units, and news headlines concerning changes in the economy and employment, and by monitoring how long it takes for your unoccupied rentals to be rented out.

A lot of small investors and management organizations adapt slowly. You can stay ahead of your rivals by looking out for trends and being innovative in getting the perfect tenants. In an economy that is slowly regrouping, investors complain that they are unable to reduce the price of a rental unit. This problem is made worse by renting to terrible tenants, or at a very high price. An increase in the rate at which your units are occupied makes your cash flow more stable.

It might be useful for you if you work together with other investors since you won't be doing the research alone. Also, you can get information from them concerning the trends they are dealing with.

Make use of Logical Procedures and Policies

Most experienced managers and investors reject tenants with criminal histories, unreliable landlord references, unstable jobs, or low credit. Most times they search for private landlords to rent from just because they could not pass the screening for qualification; thus, their rent is more expensive because of these risks. I can only keep reminding you how pertinent it is that you put down strict rules for qualification and you adhere to them strictly. In addition to protecting you from lawsuits claiming discrimination, it also helps that you stand firm in hard times.

Most tenants became homeowners as soon as interest rates reduced to the lowest rates recorded in 40 years. The remaining tenants were those that were not qualified for a mortgage and I even came across a few that I had rejected previously. Despite this large number of tenants, I fixed strict policies and stuck to them. If you become desperate and start to allow any tenant that can afford it, that is very risky.

Reinvest

Look at your neighborhood. Are there areas that are not properly taken care of? Are there dilapidated duplexes, apartment buildings or houses? Did you ever think about how this was possible? Or could it be that the properties have become old?

There is a possibility that you are looking at rental properties that are owned by investors in debt, or a person who is keen on destroying their property by carrying out little to no maintenance that is needed for the property to continue yielding profit.

Slumlords are another name for these types of investors, and they make so much profit from their investment, until the property is demolished or sold.

High grade tenants are drawn to high grade properties. If you invest in your property again by making both the interior and exterior very pleasing to the eye, you have the basic requirements to survive and grow when the market is down. While reinvesting, concentrate first on the appeal of the curb, followed by the aesthetics of the interior.

Save Some Funds

Prepare for hidden costs and upgrades by creating a fund reserve. When you are sure everything is falling into place, a major expense might come up or some of your long-term tenants might drop a relocation notice. You have to make plans and thorough preparations. Having long-term tenants means that you might spend a lot of money because you would have to renovate their unit when they relocate.

Assess Your Strategies Again

You must be able to adapt to every change in the market. A few times, there might have to be a change in the policy once there is a change in the market.

Make sure to evaluate the things that are effective and those that are not. Come up with the ways to deal with the risk and formulate written guidelines to handle the risk.

It is very important that you are consistent, however, overlooking trends is the easiest way to fail. Schedule an annual review of policies, preferably in the middle of May, or towards the end, during the tedious summer relocating season.

Assess the performance of your property (and discard the irrelevant things)

While evaluating your policies in May, you should also assess the performance of all your properties using a similar analysis to the one you used when you agreed to purchase. Contrast investment returns, examine the vacancy rates and consult your realtor for information concerning similar properties for sale. Sit with your accountant to review your tax status and the ways by which your position would be improved by your investments. Is your property yielding the expected profits or is selling it or exchanging it a smart move?

128

Always regard your rentals like a business and make choices that would be profitable for your business. A few landlords develop an attachment to their properties, and they are unable to see the long-term benefits of the investments.

There are so many opportunities. If a great deal passes you by, continue to be resilient. A good real estate agent will keep informing you about all the available options in the market, until you locate your preferred property.

If it does not sit well with you, do not purchase the property. If there is a written agreement, take your time to make sure that this investment feels right, and you are comfortable with it. Changing your mind before purchasing the property is better than changing it after. You might already be swamped with expenses.

Reacting (or otherwise) to Fluctuations in the Market

Assuming there is an increase in the rental market after you have been straining to get by and maintaining the property for the past 2-3 years. The logical thing is to make similar modifications that are being made by other landlords, with your tenants. This is the wrong time to inflate the rent of your long-term tenants. Keep in mind that you would be doing this for a long time, and keeping the right tenant is very important.

Contrarily, there might be a general reduction in the price of rent. Approach your tenants. Do not expect them to come to you for a reduction in their rent. You might not see them because they are looking for cheaper offers and by the time you discover this, it might be irreversible.

Remember that turnover is expensive and increases your expenses.

Market fluctuations provide the perfect opportunity for you to put your long-term plans into action. Avoid being narrow-minded.

Conclusion

It is almost impossible for an average person to become a rental property investor. The only way that an average individual can become an investor in the rental property business is by handling their property like a business and handling their tenant(s) with sincerity.

Now that you have all this knowledge, you should share this information with other investors. Learn how to apply these techniques and teach other people how to do so as well, so that everyone is provided with an opportunity to improve their skills in rental property investment.

A weak person will find that a rental property business is too difficult. However, for a strong person, it can yield great profits. However, you must be ready to deal with all kinds of people (tenants). This is difficult for many people. But the knowledge gained from this book can significantly improve the strategies you can use to manage your tenants and rental properties.

Is there any assurance that you will make progress? Definitely. You can increase your chances of success by putting in the effort, carrying out the research, studying the book, and putting it into practice.

The benefits are much more rewarding than you could ever imagine to be possible.

Made in the USA
Middletown, DE
07 December 2019